YOU ARE
HERE

A STRAIGHT-SHOOTING GUIDE TO
MAPPING YOUR FUTURE

YOU ARE HERE

A STRAIGHT-SHOOTING GUIDE TO MAPPING YOUR FUTURE

DANNY HOLLAND

WATERBROOK
PRESS

YOU ARE HERE
PUBLISHED BY WATERBROOK PRESS
12265 Oracle Boulevard, Suite 200
Colorado Springs, Colorado 80921
A division of Random House Inc.

All Scripture quotations, unless otherwise indicated, are taken from the Holy Bible,
New International Version®. NIV®. Copyright © 1973, 1978, 1984 by International Bible
Society. Used by permission of Zondervan Publishing House. All rights reserved. Scripture
quotations marked (ASV) are taken from the American Standard Version. Scripture quotations
marked (KJV) are taken from the King James Version. Scripture quotations marked (MSG) are
taken from The Message by Eugene H. Peterson. Copyright © 1993, 1994, 1995, 1996, 2000,
2001, 2002. Used by permission of NavPress Publishing Group. All rights reserved. Scripture
quotations marked (NASB) are taken from the New American Standard Bible ®. Copyright ©
The Lockman Foundation 1960, 1962, 1963, 1968, 1971, 1972, 1973, 1975, 1977, 1995.
Used by permission. (www.Lockman.org). Scripture quotations marked (NLT) are taken from
the Holy Bible, New Living Translation, copyright © 1996, 2004. Used by permission of
Tyndale House Publishers Inc., Wheaton, Illinois 60189. All rights reserved.

Italics in Scripture quotations indicate the author's added emphasis.

ISBN: 978-1-4000-7203-3

Copyright © 2007 by Danny Holland

Library of Congress Cataloging-in-Publication Data
Holland, Danny, 1969-
    You are here : a straight-shooting guide to mapping your future / Danny Holland. — 1st ed.
        p. cm.
    Includes bibliographical references.
    ISBN 978-1-4000-7203-3
    1. Teenagers—Religious life. 2. Self-actualization (Psychology)—Religious aspects—Christianity.
3. Self-actualization (Psychology) in adolescence. I. Title.
    BV4531.3.H65 2007
    248.8'3—dc22

                                        2007012689

Printed in the United States of America
2007—First Edition

10 9 8 7 6 5 4 3 2 1

To Joshua and Caleb

CONTENTS

SECTION 3: DESTINY

FOREWORD

Each of us gets one chance at this thing called life. Often we prepare more for a weekend athletic contest than we do for eternity. We spend more time stretching our muscles in order to decrease the probability of injury than we do to lessen the years of damage caused by poor decisions.

Danny Holland does not teach from concepts or knowledge alone (although he is very knowledgeable).

Danny teaches from scars.

And knowing that God never wastes a hurt, neither does Danny. He leaves lessons like trail markers to help others navigate successfully. He lays down his life in poignant lessons so others who read these lines may pick up their futures and live the optimum life they were designed to live.

Danny's experiences in outrigger canoes will whet your adventurous spirit. You'll ride into the open ocean and dance with the waves, and the lessons learned will add rhythm to your journey.

Follow with anticipation.

It will require humility. It will require discipline. It will require imagination.

Imagination always trumps fear. Imagination reveals what could be, and when combined with God's promises, it becomes the raw ingredient that produces great people, great futures, and the delights of a great God! So launch out. It will be an adventure filled with lessons for avid students of the beyond. And for a brief moment, look behind you. The One who is steering has been this way before, and with nail-pierced hands He pats your shoulder and whispers, "Welcome home."

—DR. WAYNE CORDEIRO, Senior Pastor
New Hope Christian Fellowship, Oahu, Hawaii

INTRODUCTION

We've all either been there, are there, or will be there—standing on the shores of the known, gazing into the waters of the deep, wondering if there is *more*. Perhaps, like me, you've felt a tug to leave the security of the known and enter the chaos of the unknown in pursuit of deeper meaning.

Each of us has been created with a special purpose. We have been uniquely fashioned for greatness, yet that greatness often eludes us. The concepts in this book will help you recognize where you are, where you are going, and how to make the right transitions through each stage of your life journey.

What do you know of your future? I don't imagine you have a map with pins marking all the major events you will one day experience. And what about all the smaller events? Do you have enough pins? The journey we call life is filled with extraordinary moments packaged in the most mundane wrappings. They may seem uneventful, but these sometimes frightening, sometimes painful moments are crucial to the completion of the assignment God has for you.

You are here. Today is the next step in your journey, and each step is crucial. The skills you learn now are essential to success along your journey.

I wrote this book to help you recognize the purpose of your life and maximize each moment. Nothing in your life has escaped God's attention. Everything you and I experience, the way we were created, and the gifts we possess can all work together to accomplish great things.

The synergy of our experiences and resources prepares us for the journey. Like a highly experienced paddling team, as we hone the key skills, we prepare for success.

Your life is part of a grand plan, and you can help make that plan happen when you cooperate with your Creator. This book will help you successfully discover and navigate how to do that—how to live the life you were meant to live.

Let the journey begin!

WHAT MAP
ARE YOU
IN?

Look

I can't explain it.

I suppose I made the decision the moment I gazed at the royal blue and turquoise water of the Hawaiian shore. As I stood in a parking lot filled with vehicles adorned with racks for canoes and wave-riding gear, I felt the salty fragrance of the ocean, the sun's gentle warmth, and the whisper of the water calling me.

I left the shore and headed into the deep.

I can do this, I thought, my eyes scanning the ocean canoes that rocked gently with each wave of the crystal sea.

No. I have *to do this.*

Passion, excitement, and a sense of destiny surged through my veins. I'd been offered a position with New Hope Christian Fellowship in Honolulu. But there was something else, something more—an inaudible voice calling me to something greater. Would I embrace the call? Or would I shrink back to the safety and comfort of my normal life?

This was the moment of truth. I had to face facts and accept my calling—suddenly, somehow, all at once. You've probably felt something like that too: times in your life when you've felt called to respond, act, and do something extraordinary.

But then something gets in the way.

Either all at once or over time, we raise barriers or develop systems to silence that little voice. We ignore it. Bury it. Drown it out. Regard it as nonsense. And we slide back into the familiar life, back to thinking *reasonably* and *responsibly.* We carefully craft logical reasons to shove the wild notions aside and begin to wonder why we ever allowed the thoughts to enter our mind in the first place. We tell ourselves to grow up, to quit being impulsive. We "hang up" on the call.

What if I had listened? What then?

• Everyone Gets One •

Without exception, every one of us gets a unique, one-of-a-kind purpose. The Bible tells us that God knows how many hairs are on our head and that, like Jeremiah, before we ever entered the world, He knew us and had plans for our lives (Luke 12:7; Jeremiah 29:11). Maybe it's not so easy to see. Maybe it's been damaged or even crushed by the heavy things we've piled up around it. A purpose can be as elusive as a tigerfish or as reclusive as a great white shark. But the truth is, our purpose is what calls us into the deep of the unknown.

A purpose can be as elusive as a tigerfish
or as reclusive as a great white shark.

As we stand on the shore with the gentle waves lapping at our feet and our backs to the road we've traveled before, we feel the pull of that purpose. We feel the call to leave the lesser dream of a gray, undiscovered life and embrace the vivid colors of a life of true purpose.

The process of determining your unique purpose isn't always easy. You will face risks, and fear will threaten to overwhelm your senses. But what are your options? Well, you can reject what God planned for your life and slip into the predictable grind…or you can embark on a lifelong, amazing, God-directed adventure.

Two maps, one journey. Which map will you follow?

• FOR THIS MOMENT •

I like to contemplate life (isn't that what Starbucks is all about?), and I know many others who enjoy standing on a metaphorical shore, staring into the unknown and pondering, *Am I ready? Do I have what I need? What if I fail?* We're pretty good at listing reasons not to get our feet wet. But what if we've spent our entire life in preparation for this moment?

Each of us is hard-wired with signature strengths and a specific, genuine personality designed for accepting our specific, genuine call. Sure, we possess our parents' DNA, but each of us is also infused with unique spiritual DNA strands stamped with our assignment from our heavenly Father. We have been thoroughly and meticulously equipped for everything we're called to do. Helping you to find your assignment is a key goal of this book. But as you prepare to respond according to your skills, talents, personality, and preferences, you will feel the surge of something bigger—something more. The call to what you were created to do isn't a distant destination. It is an everyday journey from mediocrity to excellence. The call is what turns those mundanely wrapped moments into extraordinary events.

· THE JOURNEY OF EXCELLENCE ·

This morning at Starbucks I cracked open my Bible and examined the life of Daniel. Between sips of my latte, I read about a young man who wasn't all that different from you and me. He discovered and embraced his assignment. Daniel stood at the shore of his call and then dove into the deep.

We all experience mediocrity. The word *mediocre* literally means "halfway up the mountain." It implies a moderate level of success blended with failure. Being mediocre doesn't mean your class rank is the same number as the total number of students in your class, but it doesn't mean you're the valedictorian either. It's the "good enough" life we give up the best for. Of course we can't all be the academic genius or the fastest runner, but that's no shocker. What *is* a shocker is that every one of us was created to live out an assignment that is light-years beyond mediocre. Interestingly, in the original languages of the Bible, the word *excellence* means "a mountain over the horizon standing above everything else."

This assignment is more than we can accomplish with our natural gifts and initiative. We need power. *God's* power. Our strength pales in comparison to what God can provide. The best-lived life will only reach excellence through preparation and alignment with that power—alignment with God's greater plan.

When Daniel was about fourteen years old, he was taken hostage by King Nebuchadnezzar. The famous king wasn't taking just anyone hostage but was grooming future leaders to supercharge his culture with his ideas, ideology, and standards. The king narrowed his search by selecting noblemen's sons who were handsome, bright, and well educated.

> The best-lived life will only reach excellence through
> preparation and alignment with God's greater plan.

According to the account, Daniel was "ridiculously good-looking" (to quote the eloquent Derek Zoolander) and also well prepared. Daniel awoke each day with a readiness to respond to God's call. He knew his life had value. And he knew he had important things to learn.

Then something spectacular happened to Daniel, something others would probably have considered tragic. His journey out of mediocrity, which began while he was a young boy, was about to accelerate dramatically. Daniel was about to enter the epicenter of his life assignment. And he was prepared for "such a time as this" (Esther 4:14).

For a season in history, Daniel's purpose, preparation, and gifting aligned perfectly with God's agenda and timing. The habits Daniel had practiced in obscurity became a platform that God would use to impact several regimes and even a nation. The Bible tells us that as a dream interpreter, Daniel was ten times better than all the magicians and enchanters in Nebuchadnezzar's kingdom. Daniel yielded to his assignment, which eventually led him to become the top man in the kingdom.

· THE SECRET FORMULA OF EXCELLENCE ·

Like you and me, Daniel was hard-wired for excellence. God planted gifts, signature strengths, purpose, and a personality in him to equip him for his journey. Had Daniel used these tools for personal gain, he might have become rich or achieved high status and fame. Others might have considered that a successful life. But even at his best, at the top of his game, in light of God's assignment for him—his purpose—he would have been mediocre. He was created to be a vital part of God's agenda, not just some smart, ridiculously good-looking rich guy.

While Daniel was a very young man, he discovered the tools that made him a great dream interpreter. He recognized strengths that made him stand out among others. Not only did he discover them, he also developed them to maturity. We know from the way Daniel looked, from his strict diet and prayer life, that Daniel lived a disciplined lifestyle. Through this discipline, Daniel prepared himself for future events where he would align with his purpose and achieve moments of excellence.

What motivated Daniel to live his life this way? I believe he felt a sense of destiny every day. Because he understood the importance of his life to God, even in seasons when he could have gotten away with less, he always remembered he had been created for something great.

Daniel also yielded himself to God. He surrendered his gifts to God to be used for a greater purpose.

When we participate with God in seeking excellence, we have to act in faith. If we hesitate to act, fear can paralyze us. When we look straight in the face of our life's purpose, we *will* feel fear. *What if I fail? I'm not capable of this. What if I'm wrong? What will my family think? Nobody believes I can do this.*

When we participate with God in seeking excellence,
we have to act in faith.

I am the father of two boys and have invested plenty of time teaching them to swim. There are small victories in the process, like the first time the boys put their faces in the water. Getting them to leave the side of the pool was another triumph. Every time I arrive at the pool, I am reminded of the old Coke commercial featuring a mother polar bear and her cubs. Mama patiently tries to entice a young cub into the arctic waters. She slaps the water with her paw, but the cub just backs away, groaning with fear. What's a mother polar bear to do? Here's an idea: grab a Coke! She reveals a bottle of the refreshing beverage and enticingly shows it to her cub. Separated from his mother by a small gulf of frigid water, the cub hesitates while contemplating the risk and reward. The temptation seems overwhelming. Convinced of the reward's worth, baby finally overcomes his fear and dives underwater, paddling to the ice where Mom and the Coke wait. As junior climbs out of the water, mom embraces him with pride and joy, then hands him his sweet reward.

I could have stood on the side of a pool until a glacier melted and neither of my boys would have traded their fear for a Coke. Fear can act like a lead weight anchoring your feet to the shore. Fear says:

- "Don't move. You might fail."
- "You can't do that. You'll never make it."
- "Be reasonable."
- "That's for someone else. You can do better elsewhere."

Faith, however, embraces risk and acts. Faith says:

- "You can do this with God."
- "God will intervene and help. You cannot fail."
- "Choose to trust Him. Let go!"

· FAVORED ·

When our hard-wired gifts, strengths, and abilities are honed through seasons of preparation and discipline and then dedicated to the use of a greater purpose, we are destined to collide with our God-given assignment. As Daniel experienced, when these key ingredients interact, the result is a divine reaction that the Bible describes as *favor.*

Daniel, Joseph, and Esther all experienced the phenomenon of favor. Mary, the mother of Jesus, encountered an angel who announced that she was "highly favored"—chosen to become pregnant with Jesus (Luke 1:28). When her prepared heart met her God-ordained assignment, she found great favor.

We might be tempted to believe these people achieved an elite status that's beyond us, but we must remember it's the assignment that makes the person, not the other way around. I wonder if so much of David's life would be recorded in Scripture if King Saul had not failed to fulfill *his* calling. David's assignment made him the legend. He was a shepherd boy who prepared and yielded himself to God and intersected with God's agenda. That's why we remember him as a great man.

Each of us has been
designed for excellence.

While we may not be called to greatness as our world defines it, each of us has been designed for excellence. We may try to fill that desire with material things, unhealthy relationships, fancy titles, or other alternatives, but nothing can satisfy like experiencing the divine reaction—God's favor.

No matter how arduous the reality of our earthly assignment, we must heed the call.

The moment has come. Are you ready? Then jump!

JUMP IN

1. Daniel practiced lifestyle traits in obscurity that were evident in public. What are three things you must master in your daily life that are foundational to future success?

   _____

   _____

   _____

   What two steps are you committed to taking to grow in these areas?

   _____

   _____

2. Fear paralyzes us. What are three fears that keep you from moving?

   _____

   _____

   _____

   What is one way you can combat each fear with faith?

   _____

   _____

3. Take inventory: list ways you are hard-wired—the gifts,
   strengths, and abilities God has given you. (Ask God for
   insight here.)

   _____

   _____

   _____

   _____

   _____

   _____

   Write at least one point or step of action you need to take to
   develop each of these hard-wired qualities.

   _____

   _____

   _____

   _____

   _____

   _____

2

Leap

As a young boy, I could imagine no words more exciting than these uttered by my mom and dad: "We're going to the lake."

Stuffed into a car loaded down with every conceivable water toy and accessory, our family would begin the trek from Milwaukee to Waupaca, Wisconsin, home of "the lake." My sister and I sat in the far back, rear-facing seat of the station wagon, taunting drivers behind us. After all, *we* were going to the lake.

Eventually, the highway turned into a county road, and as we neared our oasis of fun, we slipped on scuba fins, masks, and snorkels. Like Navy SEALS, we were ready to deploy immediately upon arrival.

Oh, what feelings of ecstasy to arrive at the lake!

The lake meant great food; fun times with Mom, Dad, my sister, Uncle Ted, Auntie "B," Susan, and Allen; and of course, The Boat. I loved roaring in circles around the lake in my cousin Allen's speedboat. During the times when the adults only wanted to sit and talk on the shore (which seemed to last an eternity), I captained my own boat—the splendid aluminum canoe.

I would flip that silver canoe over on the shore, kill a few lonely spiders, and gently slide her into the murky water. With a bright orange foam flotation device strapped around my skinny body and my passenger/loving mother in place, I was ready for my next grand journey.

There was nothing like the lake.

A decade passed, and after we moved, the lake was suddenly a two-day drive away. No worries: my insatiable appetite for water adventures would be fed by the Atlantic Ocean at Nags Head, North Carolina. I had traded the backseat of the station wagon for my own truck with tires so fat I could drive across the sand right to the edge of the lapping waves.

One day, while in a reflective mood, I sat on the beach facing the endless horizon and listening to hungry seagulls squawking background music. I poked my finger into the sand, and a number of grains stuck to it. I carefully wiped away every grain except one. Examining that lone speck of sand on my index finger, I had a revelation. *This is life,* I thought. *This is all I've got. One shot. One brief moment in time. It's what the Bible calls a vapor or a breath.*

I scanned up and down the shore and wondered how many grains of sand there were. Could they even be counted?

Imagine that beach with me. Stick your finger in the sand and take a look. One grain is what we have to make our mark. It's what we do with that one grain of sand that affects eternity.

This is all I've got. One shot.
One brief moment in time.

Even though we are traveling at more than 6,600 miles per hour, flying through space on a planet that is millions of years old, *this* is our time. God has strategically placed each of us on earth for this specific season. The apostle Paul acknowledged this when he wrote, "From one man he made every nation of men, that they should inhabit the whole earth; and he determined the times set for them and the exact places where they should live" (Acts 17:26).

But that's not all God has arranged. He's dropped a message into our hearts and equipped us with gifts and tools. It is vital that we each view our grain of sand in light of eternity. Many people live with their attention restricted to that one grain. They buy into a culture that tells us to do whatever makes us happy in the moment. They get caught up in the frantic pursuit of selfishly enjoying their grain for as long as they can. Like Tommy in the movie *Tommy Boy,* they pursue pleasure. They pamper their little grain of a moment—loving it, kissing it, massaging it—believing it is the most they could hope for.

God intends that we live with eternity in mind. Our purpose is far greater than any mundane cycle of meaning concocted by even the most creative mind of man. Let's unpack this together.

Most of us recognize the value of education. Imagine that you are going to college with only your *one grain* in mind. If this is your focus, college becomes merely a means of getting a good job and making a sizable salary so you can enjoy the comforts of the Western world. It becomes a steppingstone to a nice house in a sought-after neighborhood with excellent schools, a place to live that says to your neighbors, "I am successful." And where do you go from there? Well, you get married and have 1.3 kids and send them to the good schools so they can eventually get good jobs and make sizable salaries and enjoy the comforts of the Western world. The cycle repeats.

Do you think that is why God created you and put you on the earth?

Thinking in the context of eternity is about doing
your part to help others deal with pain and suffering.

Now let's revise your imaginary life. This time, think of your life with the entire beach, all of eternity, in mind. Now why are you at college? Because that education can hone your skills and help you acquire tools that you can use for the rest of your life, impacting others for God and His kingdom. Thinking in the context of eternity isn't just about the hope of heaven, but also about doing your part to help others deal with pain and suffering. With eternity in mind, we no longer worry if our neighbors are singing our praises, because in this brief moment in time, it doesn't really matter. Our eyes are locked on Jesus, who is the "author and perfecter" of the grain He has given us (Hebrews 12:2). Our only agenda is to make Him proud.

Life is about taking the message God has dropped in your heart and expressing it every waking day of your life.

· YOUR INTERNAL GPS ·

You are equipped with a built-in GPS unit. This unit is constructed from the combination of your personality and divine instruction and can lead you to your unique opportunities and ultimately to your greatest purpose. It very likely has already helped you navigate difficult terrain. Here and now, reading this book, is the moment in time you have been directed to by that GPS. Sure, some of us have taken a more scenic route than others. Some of us have ignored the unobtrusive readout at times. But this little GPS has never been surprised by any weird place we may have ended up. It is more than able to get you to your destination from *wherever* you are today.

I am amazed when I read about the early life of King David. How would you feel if a prophet asked your father to show him all of his sons so the prophet could anoint one as the future king—and your father didn't even mention you? Talk about dysfunctional. You might say that David wasn't embraced by his family.

While this drama was unfolding, David was faithfully experimenting with his GPS unit. He was learning to understand God's ways and how to do the right things for the right reasons. David was practicing with the gifts he would soon use to free his nation and fulfill his life's plan.

Perhaps you remember the story of David delivering lunch to his brothers (who were in the army). Along the way, David heard Goliath mocking God and was filled with emotion he'd felt before. Where? In the fields while shepherding sheep. In the mundane places of life, when nobody was looking. David went to Saul and asked permission to kill this champion warrior:

> David said to Saul, "Your servant has been keeping his father's sheep. When a lion or a bear came and carried off a sheep from the flock, I went after it, struck it and rescued the sheep from its mouth. When it turned on me, I seized it by its hair, struck it and killed it. Your servant has killed both the lion and the bear; this uncircumcised Philistine will be like one of them, because he has defied the armies of the living God." (1 Samuel 17:34–36)

In the obscurity of his youth, David developed skills and a heart that represented his future potential. Later in the story, David was gearing up for battle in a man's armor. It didn't fit and would have hampered him. David decided to get the job done using only his own tools, the weapons he was comfortable with. "Then he took his staff in his hand, chose five smooth stones from the stream, put them in the pouch of his shepherd's bag and, with his sling in hand, approached the Philistine" (1 Samuel 17:40).

I understand the sling and stones, but why did David bring his staff? *Dude, you're facing a heavily armed giant! A staff?* Before we question David's smarts, let's look at another confrontation reported in the Bible. God was preparing Moses to confront the Egyptian rulers and free God's people from captivity. Moses asked God a legitimate question:

"What if they do not believe me or listen to me and say, 'The LORD did not appear to you'?"

Then the LORD said to him, "What is that in your hand?"

"A staff," he replied.

The LORD said, "Throw it on the ground."

Moses threw it on the ground and it became a snake. (Exodus 4:1–3)

That trick with the snake is amazing, but it's more important to understand how significant a staff was in those times. Shepherds carried staffs to help control and discipline the sheep. During downtime, like when the sheep were happily grazing, shepherds would carve designs on their staffs. That's right—they carved pictures to remind them of great moments in their lives. Moses probably had little pictures of his history with God, maybe a burning bush. I suspect David's staff had carvings of a lion and a bear.

David entered into the battle of his life with nothing but his weapon of choice, his faith, and a reminder of the highlight moments in his life.

· TRUST ·

In one of my favorite scenes in the movie *The Karate Kid,* the kid, "Daniel-san," is completely exhausted, with two lifeless limbs hanging from his shoulders. His karate lessons from Mr. Miyagi to that point had been—how do I put it?—weird. Daniel had waxed cars and painted fences, and in a moment of frustration, he finally exploded at his teacher. After Mr. Miyagi brought life back to the kid's arms, he showed Daniel how painting the fence and waxing cars had trained his muscles to react to various attacks. Humbled by the revered teacher's wise training, Daniel walked away with eyes wide open.

Some of the more significant things in life happen in the mundane seasons. Sometimes the journey seems to be taking forever. We long for the moment when we will rise to greatness but often fail to realize that greatness is a process. For most of us, that future greatness is a seed germinating in the decisions and habits we develop today. As we plod along our course, climbing over obstacles, we whittle memories on our staff: Parents divorced. Leadership in youth group. Missions trip. Learned to play the guitar. Little by little our staff accumulates the carvings of our "lions" and "bears."

We take what is in our hands
and turn to face the giant warrior.

From time to time, a towering Goliath will confront us. We take what is in our hands—the experiences we've accumulated, God's answers to our prayers, our faith, our skills, our abilities—and turn to face the giant warrior.

Then, and only then, does the grain of sand make sense. For a brief moment, the course our GPS has led us on intersects with an opportunity to impact eternity.

• WET FEET •

Back on the shore...

I met and embraced my appetite for water at a small lake in Wisconsin. In the Atlantic off the coast of North Carolina, I developed and honed my skills and grew confidence to face rougher waters. Now, as I stand at the Pacific Ocean with water lapping at my feet, my excitement brews.

Like the grand water adventure awaiting me, the greatness looming on *your* horizon depends on experiences you have already navigated. Yet experience alone is not enough to prepare you and me for excellence.

The same experiences that have the power to shape and equip us for future adventures can also hinder us. We need to manage our lives and develop our character to get the maximum benefit from each experience. We need to understand that it's not always in the calmer waters that we become equipped for the bigger waves.

Imagine you're sixty-five years old. You have risen to the top of your career field. You have done well by many standards. You've prepared for retirement and can live well off of your investments. Turn around and look behind you. What do you see? What have you done with your grain of sand?

Solomon was one of the wisest men to ever live. Wives, riches, power, prestige—King Solomon had it all. Near the end of his life, Solomon did exactly what you and I just imagined doing. He turned around. He examined everything he had considered important. He studied the productivity of all he had sought and valued. His assessment is surprising:

"Meaningless! Meaningless!"
    says the Teacher.
"Utterly meaningless!
    Everything is meaningless."
What does man gain from all his labor
    at which he toils under the sun?

Generations come and generations go,

    but the earth remains forever. (Ecclesiastes 1:2–4)

What will *we* say? What if we felt a call to missions and never went? What if we sought pleasure instead of the message God implanted into our hearts? Jesus asked a rhetorical question when He said, "And what do you benefit if you gain the whole world but lose your own soul? Is anything worth more than your soul?" (Matthew 16:26, NLT). When Jesus asks, the answer seems like a no-brainer. But how often do we turn our backs on the difficult road that leads toward our God-given purpose and follow the path of greatest ease?

One of my mentors, Wayne Cordeiro, once said, "If leisure or pain-less living is your goal, you will be paralyzed and useless." I know I don't want to look back on my life and prove the accuracy of that statement. Throughout your life, you will choose one of two roads. The first is wide and well traveled and leads to mediocrity. The other, the less-traveled road, leads to excellence and greatness. As you choose your path, remember that God never designed you to live life in the gray but rather to experience the vivid colors of the highs and the lows of life and to make your mark along the way.

• WHERE LIFE WAS MEANT TO BE LIVED •

The less-traveled road is less traveled for a reason: it's difficult, paved with failure and hardship. But its reward is greatness and eternal value. What kind of a swimmer do you think you'd be today if you never gave up the water wings or took off the life vest? To pursue your purpose and live a life of excellence, you need to be able to swim out into the deeper waters. The more demanding the circumstances, the more refined you will emerge.

Surviving life's difficulties changes us. When we maintain a healthy lifestyle and attitude, struggles can propel us into greatness and bring our lives from mild mediocrity to exceptional excellence. Some of the greatest heroes in the Bible went through seasons when they were in over their heads.

What kind of a swimmer do you think you'd
be today if you never gave up the water wings?

I think of Joshua, an emerging leader in Israel. Early in his life, he was selected to join a group of spies and check out the land of Canaan to see if the Israelites could inhabit it successfully. Only Joshua and Caleb looked with a positive, faith-filled attitude at the difficulty of conquering this land. Only Joshua and Caleb opted for the less-traveled, difficult road to greatness.

Unfortunately, the rest of the spies chose the wider path, and the nation was doomed to wander in the desert for forty more years. God promised them they would never see Canaan because of their poor attitude and lack of trust in Him. Their decision to avoid getting in over their heads cost them everything. They spent the remainder of their lives roaming around a desert in the gray of life. Joshua and Caleb, however, got to see the dazzling colors of life as they led a new generation through the difficult path into God's promised place.

It is in our weakness that God is strongest. The journey God has planned for you is one of ups and downs. And here's something important to understand: that journey is not *to* a destination—it *is* the destination. Along the path is where our Creator reveals Himself to us and unveils the assignment hidden in each of our hearts. God's plans require that we be in over our heads. It is in those moments that time and purpose intersect with God's intervention and create spectacular adventures beyond anything we could experience alone.

· YOU GET WHAT YOU PAY FOR ·

A legacy of greatness awaits each of us in the vivid colors of our purpose. But there is a price to pay if our seemingly insignificant grains of sand are to stand out on the beaches of eternity. The price we pay often determines the level of greatness we achieve. Every time we stand on the shore and scan the challenges on the horizon, we have to make a choice. When we accept the price, set our face toward the horizon, and face the challenges before us, we step off the widely traveled road and onto the path to greatness we were created to walk.

JUMP IN

1. If you were the proverbial shepherd and were given a new staff, what would you carve on it?

_____

_____

_____

_____

2. Imagine retiring and looking back at your life. What will you hope to have accomplished?

_____

_____

_____

3. From time to time we must take off our "water wings" in order to leap. What are the safety devices you may need to get rid of?

_____

_____

_____

_____

Seek

3

"Okay, men!" the steersman shouted. "It's go time!"

I snapped awake from a daydream of summer days at the lake. I heard the far-off whitecaps curling on the horizon. Calm and confident, I felt ready for the adventure.

Step out, Danny. Come experience life in the deep.

I picked up my paddle and helped push the half-ton vessel off the rocky shore into the peaceful lagoon, jumping—rather gracefully, I thought—into seat five.

Wow, this is much more stable than Uncle Ted's canoe. The ama, a long arm that floats on the left side of the enormous sea kayak to balance it, provided peace of mind as we skimmed briskly across the surface of the teal water. The steersman at the rear barked out commands. The men in seats one and two began to dip their paddles in perfect cadence. Three and four followed their lead, with me in seat five, doing my best to match the rhythm of the team. The vessel surged through the motionless water, bubbles circling my paddle's blade as I plunged and thrust with forceful strokes.

The muscles in my arms and shoulders began to swell, just like during an intense workout at the gym. After about ten minutes, the canoe slowed as the steersman behind me in seat six began a slow turn. Our trip appeared to be ending as we headed back toward the beach. My pride swelled—I was the tough white guy from the mainland who never quit paddling hard. My Hawaiian paddlers didn't seem interested in my celebratory camaraderie. I did want to go out farther, but my muscles were a bit numb. I prepared to exit the canoe.

Words can't describe the horror I felt when I realized the boat was slowly trolling past our home beach and heading toward the inlet of the placid lagoon. The voyage so far? Merely a warmup.

"Paddles up!" the steersman suddenly ordered. The intensity of the command was just enough motivation for me to lift what felt like a two-ton paddle over my head. I had been in the canoe only fifteen minutes, but my arms felt rubbery and useless.

"Hit!" I heard, and the trained athletes pounded their paddles into the water. I too began paddling for all I was worth—about three-tenths of a second slower than everyone else.

We neared the mouth of the inlet. Beyond, the Pacific waited.

· WHY AM I HERE? ·

The inner voice that had so enthusiastically encouraged me on my journey into the deep was silent. My arms ached, but I had more important issues to ponder. The splashes I saw hundreds of yards out at sea, the rhythmic swells, were amazingly deep. These topped my list of worries. That is, until I noticed the fine white line on the horizon: waves.

I'm not talking about small breaking waves that swell and crash. I'm talking about humongous waves with man-sized tunnels and seawater spraying off their backs like a torrential rain. What had looked so intriguing and beautiful from the shore was now fiercely intimidating, and this boat was not turning back anytime soon. We were going to take on those waves.

What am I doing here?

When you step off the shore of mediocrity and navigate toward greatness, you will be challenged to your core. You may question even the foundation of your life, asking, *Why am I here?*

> When you step off the shore of mediocrity and navigate toward greatness, you will be challenged to your core.

Foundations are extremely important. I once heard an attorney tell a story that illustrates this truth. His client was contracted to clear the dirt on a large lot where a high-rise condominium was to be built. The job also involved trucking in a different type of dirt better suited for creating a stable foundation. The client decided that instead of replacing the existing dirt, he would simply recycle it and compact it tightly to provide what he believed would be the necessary support. The foundation was poured and the building constructed. Soon tenants filled the beautiful new units.

Not too long after occupancy, the high-rise started sliding off its foundation. Engineers quickly concluded that the building was in danger of collapse. They examined the foundation and determined that the building was not built on the right type of soil. The contractor's decision to reuse the dirt had endangered many people and cost him dearly.

We can't build our skyscraper lives on cheap dirt. The level of greatness we can achieve in life is directly related to the foundation we lay. Excellence is the fruit of preparation and cooperation with God's plan. We can't push off the shore into the deep on our momma's faith. If we don't own for ourselves the solid foundation of faith in God, the greatness we were created for will lean and may even crumble.

Jesus illustrated this concept when He said, "And no one pours new wine into old wineskins. If he does, the wine will burst the skins, and both the wine and the wineskins will be ruined" (Mark 2:22). We each have a specific assignment from God that requires our cooperation. We must prepare the wineskin that will hold that assignment. When we form our new wineskin, God can fill it with new wine.

The question is, will our core foundation support the greatness that we were created for?

Successful people have something in common with successful buildings. Success in life involves the skill of making thousands of small decisions correctly. None of us gets by without making some wrong choices.

But if we make sure our foundation is rock solid, our daily choices will increasingly be good ones.

· FOUNDATION CHECK ·

Whether we realize it or not, everyone has a core foundation in life. This core helps us solve moral dilemmas and navigate through the toughest of choices. More often than not, our decisions are in complete harmony with our core foundation. This foundation is built upon those deepest beliefs, no matter how true or false, that we hold about the makeup of our world. The question is, will our core foundation support the greatness that we were created for? Will it sustain us when our arms are numb and we still have a lot of paddling to do?

There are seven big questions we can ask to see what kind of foundation we have.

· THE UNAVOIDABLE QUESTIONS ·

These questions are important, because the battle for any generation comes at the core foundation.

The Big Seven

- What is really real?
- What is the nature of the world around us?
- What is a human being?
- What happens to a person at death?
- Can we know anything?

- How do we know what's right and wrong?
- What is the meaning of human history?

What is really real? Today on many of our college campuses, this question is answered by whatever we choose to articulate. Some people believe that God created the world, and some believe that there is nothing real beyond the seen world. Many believe that each of us is our *own* reality. In their view, for those who believe in God and heaven, heaven is real and good, but for those who don't believe in God, heaven doesn't exist. Can you see how building your life on a faithless foundation would threaten your ability to sustain anything of eternal purpose?

The answer to this question most consistent with Scripture is that God is real. He is infinite and personal, sovereign and good, and active in the affairs of men and women. When we believe this answer, our daily decisions take on new and greater meaning.

What is the nature of the world around us? While some may believe nature *is* God or that God created the world and then went away to leave us alone, these views are not consistent with Scripture. The idea that is most consistent with a biblically based core foundation is that God created the world from nothing to operate by its own natural forces working in conjunction.

What is a human being? There are many schools of thought on this question. Some teach that humans are chemical organisms that evolved from other organisms. Others teach that nobody can actually understand what a human being truly is. The biblically based core foundation that best answers this question is that humans are eternal beings created in the image of God. We have personality, creativity, intelligence, and morality. Humans have the capacity to accomplish good works. Long ago man fell out of perfect relationship with God. Jesus Christ came to earth and died to redeem humanity and restore the opportunity for each of us to once again have a righteous relationship with God. Each human being was born first in the heart of God and has a specific purpose on earth.

What happens to a person at death? Many people believe that human beings have the same fate as every other living thing on earth—they die and decay. They believe that this grain of sand called life is all there is. The biblically based core foundation answer to this question is that death is a gate either to eternal life with God and other believers or to permanent separation from God.

Can we know anything? Some belief systems claim that we can't know *anything* absolutely and that truth is situational or relative. According to this sort of thinking, individuals must determine "truth" for themselves. According to the Bible, human beings can know about the world around them and know God Himself, because God created each of us with the capacity to understand such knowledge. Not only do we have the capacity but God takes an active role in communicating truth to us.

The Bible shows us God's heart.

How do we know what's right and wrong? In the Western world, many people believe that ethics are manmade and thus do not apply equally to everyone. In this view all persons have a unique code of right and wrong. That code is their morality, and there is no universal standard of right or wrong. This idea makes personal belief supreme and provides an unstable foundation for life. Although Scripture tells us that we have a free will, we are also equipped with a conscience that gives us an ethical guide for living a life pleasing to God. That guide isn't enough, however, so God provided us with written instructions in the Bible that show us right and wrong. The Bible also shows us God's heart, what He loves and hates. It helps us develop a foundation that will support the greatness we were created for.

What is the meaning of human history? Many believe history is a string of disconnected events that have no unifying purpose. But in God's eyes, history is a string of interconnected events that are meaningful and lead toward the fulfillment of God's purposes for humanity. When we build our core foundation on this belief, we prepare to make our mark on history.

The more intentionally we shape our core foundation with biblical answers to these questions, the more stable it becomes. If we randomly construct our foundation based on cultural trends, it will be weak.

We all have the best of intentions, and everyone wants a happy ending. But good intentions are not enough. Men and women who have achieved a history-shaping life of eternal greatness learned to move beyond good intentions to good decisions. And their decisions were the outcome of a life built on biblically solid answers.

• FISHING FOR GREATNESS •

Let's examine a different picture of this.

For deep-sea fishermen, the grand prize is the elusive marlin, a sleek and powerful fish. When a marlin jumps out of the water, time seems to stand still as the sunlight glistens off the shiny skin and fan-shaped dorsal fin. It is a scene of inspiring beauty.

A story is told of two friends who went fishing for the illustrious marlin.

As they approached their fishing spot, they each prepared their bait. One man could hardly wait to get his hook in the water. Visions of a record catch were floating through his mind as he grabbed a chunk of dead meat and impaled it on the hook. The whine of the reel broke the silence as he unwound his line into the sea. His friend was anxious to fish too but took his time preparing his bait *just so* to attract a marlin. He based his preparation on tips from his fishing mentors and lessons from past experience.

Forty-five minutes later, the fish
exploded through the surface
of the water fifty yards behind the boat.

Within minutes the first friend had a bite, and he fastened himself into the chair to do battle with his catch. For hours he struggled with the fish to see who would tire first. The vision of a marlin breaking the surface was enough to keep him going in spite of the pain. Excitement grew, and finally the fight came to an end. The men gathered around as the fish neared the boat. Here it was, the moment they were waiting for. With a final burst of energy, the exhausted angler pulled the fish close enough for the boat crew to haul it in. A flounder flopped onto the deck. Hearts sank. The exhausted fisherman, now sapped of strength and energy, was so disappointed. Done for the day, he stepped down from the chair to rest.

His friend, finally finished with his bait preparation, cast his line into the water. As excited as he was to get a catch, doubt plagued him. Then something hit his hook. *I sure hope this isn't a flounder,* he thought. As he strapped himself into the chair, the battle began. Forty-five minutes later, the fish exploded through the surface of the water fifty yards behind the boat. There it was, a glistening blue marlin. Filled with new energy, the fisherman fervently battled. "A marlin. I've got a marlin!" he whispered to himself. A few hours later, the battle was over and he had captured a trophy fish.

Both of these fishermen wanted to hook a marlin. The difference was that one spent more time on preparation. He carefully considered what his mentors and wisdom had taught him. The other carelessly went through the motions.

It's important to note that not all roads lead to a happy place. We can't make random right and left turns and end up at Disneyland. Those who map out their way and lay a biblically solid foundation that supports God's great plan are the ones who will survive the deep.

JUMP IN

1. Are there any foundations in your life built on recycled dirt? If so, what steps do you need to take to rebuild them so they will support greatness?

_____

_____

_____

_____

_____

_____

2. Good intentions are not enough. List several areas in your life you want to improve.

_____

_____

_____

_____

_____

_____

For each area you listed, write the steps you need to take to achieve your intentions.

_____

_____

_____

_____

_____

_____

_____

4

Find

They were huge.

Not the waves. Those were behind us now. Somehow I'd tempted fate and survived, calling up strength and stamina I didn't realize I had. But what had been blips of color on the horizon were now larger than life—and coming toward us.

These, I learned, were navigational buoys. Passing within a few feet of such enormous floating markers, I found it difficult to comprehend that only moments earlier they were barely visible. *How far out are we?* As I paddled in cadence with the rest of the crew, I had no choice but to trust the sixth member of our crew, the steersman.

When we launch into the deep, we are forced to navigate life with precision to arrive at the desired destination. Our final goal may not even be visible from where we are, but there are markers to guide us in the right direction, helping us to avoid the hazards that exist all around us. Sometimes it may seem as if we should have stayed in the safe waters and not taken the risk. But that risk wasn't for the sake of risk. It was for a much greater cause.

• PLOT YOUR COURSE WITH PURPOSE •

Nothing in your life will bring you greater satisfaction and bring God greater glory than living out your purpose. We were designed to leave our greatest mark on earth through the fulfillment of that purpose. The cry of our culture is to be adequate—get by and enjoy life while you can. The cry of our purpose is to become exceptional. Unlike gifts, which need to be honed and developed, purpose is a *direction* we move in. It is the calling on our lives. *Purpose* is more than a buzzword or a catchy concept. It answers the big questions and the "whys" of our life. Purpose infuses substance into every activity. The greatest tragedy we can experience in life is not death but living life without knowing and fulfilling our purpose.

Finding your purpose is the key to unlocking the mystery of why you are here.

Remember the alarming discovery made by one of the most successful men in history? He looked at the lives of people who were *not* living out of their deepest purpose and said, "Everything is meaningless" (Ecclesiastes 1:2).

Purpose protects individuals and cultures. King Solomon wrote, "Where there is no vision, the people cast off restraint" (Proverbs 29:18, ASV). The *why* behind the *what* keeps us from paddling in circles without direction. Understanding that God created us for a greater purpose makes all the difference.

Finding your purpose is the key to
unlocking the mystery of why you are here.

When a strong, lifelong marriage is a part of your future, the idea of remaining abstinent takes on new meaning. When I was a young youth pastor, my heart was filled with great dreams and expectations of what God would do through my ministry and life. I often thought about the adventure that lay in wait for my future wife and me.

My search for a wife certainly wasn't without a few bumps in the road. I recall meeting one young lady who attended a reputable church and Christian school. She enjoyed discussing ministry and seemed to share many of the same life dreams I had. As a young, single man of God, I thought, *Maybe she is the one.* I decided to explore our relationship further by continuing our conversation at a restaurant the next day.

A few days after our friendly lunch chat, I received an unusual phone call. This young lady was anxious for me to come over to her house. She told me that her parents were gone and began to describe some of the activities we could engage in while they were away. Instead of temptation, offense came over me. How could she openly attack my ministry, trying to get me to engage in activities that would separate me from God? I told her never to call me again.

Two weeks later, her mother called me. "I know what my daughter told you on the phone," she said. "I'm calling to apologize." I doubted she knew exactly what I'd been told, but then she went on to say that her daughter had found out days earlier she was pregnant and "was looking for a good man to blame for the baby." Do you see how one moment with her could have affected the fulfillment of my purpose? It was God's protection and knowing the greatness of my purpose that kept me from that potential disaster.

Everything in life has a purpose (Romans 11:36). The fulfillment of our purpose does more than just fulfill us; it allows us to partner with the kingdom of God to make an impact on earth for eternity.

You and I are a reward to others, just as David was a reward to his nation (see Acts 13:36). In the book of Judges, God's people cried out for someone to deliver them from King Eglon, so God gave them Ehud (Judges 3). Queen Esther, walking in her purpose, became an answer to prayer for her people. The very fact that you are sucking air and walking on the surface of the earth is proof that your generation needs something only you can provide.

Long before we stood on the shore of our journey, God mapped out our course. Cultural dynamics were set in motion to help us develop our unique abilities. Divine appointments with key people were scheduled before we took our first breath. The Master Craftsman equipped us with skills and provided influences that would shape us into vessels that could navigate the unknown course ahead.

God designed you and me long before we hit the surface of the earth. God knew the needs of our generation. He carefully drew out the plans for a one-of-a-kind solution. He implanted all of this into your design and prepared you for arrival in your mother's womb. God was so meticulous that He created you genetically perfect to complete every great work He intended for you to do. God spoke about this process in a conversation with a prophet named Jeremiah: "Before I formed you in the womb I knew you, before you were born I set you apart; I appointed you as a prophet to the nations" (Jeremiah 1:5). Like Jeremiah, you and I were set apart and appointed before we ever entered our mother's wombs.

• IT'S IN THERE •

Locked inside each of us is the potential for eternal greatness. As a young adult, you may not be able to recognize that potential, but it's in there. Don't be quick to sell yourself short by limiting your potential greatness.

I am reminded of one young man who didn't seem capable of accomplishing much. He was born into a culture of death, defeat, and discouragement. This boy never knew his father, and his mother had abandoned him as an infant. He was raised in a racist environment and suffered from an identity crisis. He tried to lead once but utterly failed. His murder of a man led to rejection by his family. Maybe you've heard of him. His name was Moses. Like you and me, Moses had potential locked deep within him, and his purpose only became clear over a long period of time.

His murder of a man led to rejection by his family.
His name was Moses.

Moses was brought into this world to be the deliverer of God's people. While Moses was a young man, some of that potential surfaced. One day

Moses witnessed the beating of a Hebrew slave. He intervened, causing the death of an Egyptian. Although many viewed Moses as a murderer, this act was a hint of God's purpose for him coming to the surface. Was God's plan for Moses to knock off the Egyptians one by one? No. But God's plan was for Moses to stand up for His people.

Like the craftsman of a custom vessel, God sees us as finished, polished, and able to handle the most extreme waters. Hebrews 4:3 says, "His works were finished from the foundation of the world" (NASB). The fulfillment of our purpose isn't automatic. Even though our purpose is hard-wired in our souls, we still need to discover and refine it. We can't leave our future to chance. We must choose to participate with God in the process of fulfilling that purpose. Purpose gives meaning and hope to our lives as well as helps us to manage our time and other resources.

Oftentimes we are blinded to this valuable gift that lies inside of us. God's desire is to release that gift into the world. We must be careful not to let our weaknesses, shortcomings, and inabilities shape our future. When these forces influence us, we become defensive and restrict our potential. We must tap into our purpose and the gifts we possess so we can have the maximum amount of influence on our world. Recognizing our unique design is an important part of that process.

God takes great pleasure in you. The Bible tells us that God created everything, and it is for His pleasure that all things were created (Revelation 4:11). When we use the abilities that He has given us, we are literally worshiping Him. If you have an ability to dance, you can use that gift as a form of worship. If you are artistic, you can use your talent to bring God pleasure. Maybe you love children. You can pour your life into a child and bring great glory to God. When you begin living the plan God created you for, all of heaven takes notice and God is deeply satisfied.

• YOUR RACE •

We each have a race to run. Our purpose is that race. In Hebrews 11 we read about many great men and women of the faith. All of them ran their race with excellence. They were ordinary men and women who accomplished extraordinary feats. Joseph, Abraham, Moses's parents, Noah, Rahab—the list goes on and on. These people were no more special than you or I. They simply lived their lives in cooperation with God's plans.

• HERE'S THE TWIST •

We need to understand that we don't choose our purpose. The Creator creates, and as His creation, we *discover.* Here are some clues to help you discover your purpose.

What upsets you? What makes you cry? What fills your mind and heart with compassion? When you can consistently answer these three questions, you will be on your way to discovering your purpose. It is highly likely that what you sincerely care about is something that can give purpose to your gifts.

What makes you livid? What injustice or action really gets you fired up? The answers to these questions may point you toward something God can use you and your gifts to transform. You are not expected to confront every inconsistency and injustice in this culture with equal passion. Some injustices stir more passion than others, which can prompt and empower you to engage with stronger fervor.

What kinds of things make you feel most alive? This may be something that you do, talk about, or teach others how to do—but no matter what it is, when you do this thing, you walk away fulfilled and more excited about life than when doing anything else.

Many young adults pursue educational pathways and careers that are drudgeries. Some feel like round pegs stuffed into square holes. These people are constantly in survival mode, trying to keep their heads above water in an area of life that may not be the best fit. When round-peg people find their special round hole role, the result is a life defined by creativity, energy, and excellence.

When round-peg people find their
round hole, the result is a life of creativity,
energy, and excellence.

What do you feel must be done with excellence? God designed each of us to see our purpose accomplished well. Do you notice something not being done as well as it could be? Your hunger for excellence is an indication of strong passion in that area.

What kind of hero are you? Are you a leader in every group you join? Do you take charge? Are you motivational, always lifting the spirits of those around you? Or are you a quiet warrior?

I have two sons who are drastically different. One weekend I was preparing to do some yard work, and my oldest son asked me if he could help. He loves to take on projects and accomplish tasks.

"Dad, can I edge the driveway?" Josh asked.

"Sure," I responded, getting the edger out of the garage. After I began cutting the grass, I soon lost sight of him. When I returned to the garage to refill the mower's gas tank, I noticed Josh supervising a work crew of neighborhood friends. Some had brooms, some had other tools, but all were working hard cleaning up after Josh's edging job. Josh hurried over to me and asked, "Dad, can I get some money and pay them?"

Josh has a verbal leadership gift, and he is at his best when recruiting others and giving motivation and instructions.

My other son, Caleb, can best be described as a compassionate warrior. Even when we horseplay around the house, Caleb is always rescuing the underdog. He's more serious than the rest of us, tenaciously righting wrongs and correcting injustices. He will compassionately bend down to shake a baby's hand without concern for what his peers might think. He is fascinated with the last three days of Christ's life and cannot be separated from his Passion of the Christ spike necklace. There is no question that my boys both have the makings to be heroes in their generation, yet in very different ways.

It's important to not let the wrong influences steer our passion and gifts away from their intended purpose. Instead, we need to allow the strength of our purpose to direct our preparation.

· WHAT ARE YOUR BUOYS? ·

You are the only person who can steer your life into its purpose. When you are steering well, every day brings you a little closer to the excellence you were created for. When rough water comes, knowing where to steer can become a challenge. But when you stay focused on your God-given purpose, those specks on the horizon slowly become huge navigational markers that help you know where to turn.

The Molokai Hoe is the largest paddling competition in Hawaii. Every year more than a thousand canoe paddlers from around the globe compete in a forty-one-mile open-ocean race. Competitors launch from the island of Molokai, cross the Kaiwi Channel, and finish at the shores of Waikiki on the island of Oahu. The Kaiwi Channel can be one of the most treacherous spans of ocean in the world. In the open sea, the steersman points the canoe in the general direction of Oahu, but the ocean swells are fifteen feet or larger, so keeping the horizon visible is, to say the least, difficult.

You are the only one who can
steer your life into its purpose.

Oahu has some incredible mountains, including the infamous Diamond Head crater that towers with awe-inspiring majesty. As paddlers near the other side of the channel, Diamond Head is only a tiny dot on the horizon. Yet when standing next to the towering mountain, it's difficult to imagine anything so massive reduced to a mere dot.

Along the path of our assignment from God, He provides navigational markers to let us know we're on the right track. Some are enormous—like Diamond Head—but from our vantage point they may appear as tiny dots in the distance. All of these markers provide us with valuable insight to direct us toward the life we're created to live. If we are savvy steersmen, we slip our paddles into the water and make slight correcting adjustments according to these markers, refining the vessel's progress toward the desired destination.

An essential ingredient in the process of navigating toward our purpose is *progress.* No matter how insignificant it may seem, progress is a source of stability. Not only does progress bring us stability, it also brings balance. We need forward movement in our lives.

Consider riding a bike. Is it easier to balance on that bike while sitting still or moving? Moving, of course. You may not know exactly what the master plan is for your life, but you probably do sense that where you are today isn't the end of the journey—that you have some distance to travel. The question is, are you making progress? Even if you're just scrubbing toilets, you are traveling. You are developing a servant's heart. You are developing skills that will bring the next navigational buoy into view.

When we allow our current circumstances to shape us positively as we head in the direction of our purpose, we gain stability. When we do what we know is right and trust what God wants to do with us, we gain another added benefit: *joy* in the journey.

The Bible says, "The mind of man plans his way, but the LORD directs his steps" (Proverbs 16:9, NASB). God uses our steps (progress) to direct us. If we stand still, what can God direct? As we make forward progress, God can take us into the wild unknown of our true potential. This is where life was meant to be lived.

JUMP IN

1. What do you do that brings reward to others?

_____

_____

_____

_____

2. What God-given gifts or abilities do you have that make you special?

_____

_____

_____

_____

3. We must cooperate with God to prepare our gifts and abilities. What are some areas of life where you need to submit to God?

_____

_____

_____

_____

4. How can you take action in those areas and partner with God?

PASSION ASSESSMENT/INVENTORY

🐢 What makes you cry?

_____

_____

_____

_____

_____

🐢 What brings out your greatest compassion?

_____

_____

_____

_____

_____

🐢 Who has had the greatest influence on you and why?

_____

_____

_____

_____

_____

🐢 What injustices fire you up?

_____

_____

_____

_____

🐢 What makes you feel most alive?

_____

_____

_____

_____

🐢 What do you feel must be done with excellence?

_____

_____

_____

_____

🐢 What kind of a hero are you?

_____

_____

_____

_____

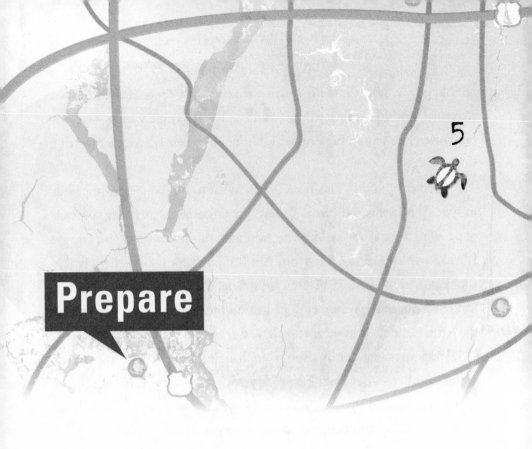

5

Prepare

*S*eat five? Why am I in seat five? It's a boat. Just put me in a seat and give me a paddle. We lined up to race. I quickly sized up the occupants of the other canoes. Canoe 1 was filled with what looked like a crew of eighteen-year-old Olympic athletes, each with a washboard stomach and shoulders directly connected to their heads. *There's no way we'll beat them,* I thought. *And how 'bout those old guys in Canoe 3?* Each one of these six looked old enough to be my father. How *special* it was to have an "old guy" canoe. *Certainly we can take them.* My canoe had a seasoned steersman and four other strong paddlers. Don't get me wrong—we certainly weren't the number one seed, but neither were we tourists wearing water wings.

"Paddles up. Hit!" This time I knew what to do. We began to paddle in sync. With arms and blades flailing, we unleashed a splashing spectacle of paddling fury. How could we not win with this much effort and energy? I broke my attention away from paddling and looked to the left. No shocker there—Canoe 1 had started strong. Those guys looked like they had come out of the womb with paddles in their hands. Then I glanced to the right. Canoe 3, with near effortless ease, was gliding ahead of everyone. The youngsters, with great effort, were hanging in there with the relaxed senior paddlers—but only barely. Our canoe now appeared more like something paddled by those water-wing–wearing tourists. Clearly it took more than strength or desire to win a canoe race.

With arms and blades flailing, we unleashed
a splashing spectacle of paddling fury.

When we break our attention off our own efforts and abilities, we can lose our identity. This is true in the pursuit of purpose. We risk losing our identity when we compare ourselves to others or allow our inadequacies to speak with the loudest voice. Satan will do whatever it takes to prevent us from stepping into our true identity. Our enemy wants to destroy our future. Many adults realize too late that they have fallen victim to his plans and deceptions.

A haphazard pursuit of purpose can also lead to the loss of identity. When the pursuit of our purpose goes off course, we lose the "why" behind what we do. When we don't understand our purpose, we misuse or abuse our gifts, time, money, and other resources. Simply stated, this means using something in a manner that isn't in accordance with its creator's purpose. If you have spent time around young children, you've probably seen this concept in action. For some reason, children (and more than a few college students) feel the need to explore "other options" for every object they can touch. Let me show you what I mean. Here are a just a few of the things I've had to say to my sons about misuse or abuse:

- "The dog is not a horse and cannot be ridden."
- "That is a ceiling fan, not a baseball bat."
- "The miniblind string is not a Tarzan swing."

I read an interesting rule at one college in Virginia. The rule stated in no uncertain terms that cafeteria trays were only for carrying food and were not to be used for riding down the campus's steep hills, no matter how much snow is on the ground.

If we don't discover our Creator's intended purpose for us, we are likely to corrupt what we have been given for accomplishing that purpose. God has equipped each of us with exactly what we need to accomplish everything He's asked us to do. How effectively we use that equipment depends on our preparation, seasons of development, and learning.

Imagine John Mayer without any musical training. The years he spent preparing his gifts are evident in his craft. What we do with our resources is up to us. The Bible teaches that before we can be entrusted with much, we must first be faithful with what little we have.

I believe each of us is perfectly crafted for everything God has planned for us. Some of us may have physical or mental limitations, but if we focus on those limitations as excuses to avoid the pursuit of our purpose, we jeopardize our identities. We need to trust that God has given us just what we need—that it's all there in our core. Of course, what we do with that core determines how we fulfill or reject our purpose.

In Numbers 13, we read the account of God's conversation with Moses about the land He was giving to the Israelites. God clearly told Moses that He was giving Canaan to them. It was a done deal. God instructed Moses to send out spies into the land. Why would spies be necessary to receive a gift from God? Even though the land was going to be given to them, God still demanded that they contend for it, strategizing and formulating their participation in the victory.

God does not rely on us to fulfill our purpose for our lives any more than He will allow us to sit back comfortably and drop it in our laps. He demands that we prepare, strategize, and contend for the very gifts that only He could give us. Think of the book of Joshua. Very little time is taken in the book describing the gift. Canaan is certainly mentioned and, toward the end, the inheritance of each tribe is discussed. But the bulk of the book is about the journey, that is, God's miraculous intervention in the plans and actions of His people. It is our cooperation with God that is so special to Him and often the most memorable for us upon arrival at our destination.

It is crucial that we respond correctly. As Numbers records, ten of the twelve spies came back to report their doubt about God's ability to fulfill His people's purpose. This doubt spread through the people like a viral epidemic. We must realize that God has good gifts for us along the path of each of our lives. He has a mate He is preparing who will exceed everything we have believed for. He has experiences planned to share with us that will bring tears of joy to our eyes and infuse our lives with purpose beyond anything we could think or even imagine. But we must be very careful that we use everything within us to cooperate with those plans.

We can destroy our potential as easily as we can hone and perfect it. I wonder how many great musical artists, moviemakers, animators, writers, and speakers didn't discover or pursue their Creator's purpose. I know of one gifted professional athlete who has had several incidents involving violence and drug abuse. A multimillionaire, he leases more than thirty exotic vehicles and allows his friends and acquaintances to drive them. He has no idea where these vehicles are and just pays the bills. What if he discovered his true identity and used his talent, influence, and money to fuel a God-directed purpose instead of his own pursuit of pleasure?

> We can destroy our potential
> as easily as we can hone and perfect it.

The hunger to know our God-given assignment is the fuel for progress. As we observe the navigational markers and find stability in our progress, we gain the ability to resist the misuse or abuse of our resources. We spend our time and money differently. Our relationships gain a new level of vitality and purpose. Our energy is spent on forward progress and the development of our gifts.

This reminds me of that fateful day I stepped off the sandy shore into seat five on our six-man canoe. Each seat in the canoe has a different job that calls for a different strength. The paddler in seat one sets the paddling pace for the team. He may be able to maintain a faster pace than what is being set for the team but he must hold the pace at a rate that maximizes the strengths of the rest of the team. Paddler number two must be able to paddle in sync with number one without watching him. Seats one and two paddle as one on opposite sides of the canoe and also switch sides in sync. The paddler in seat three follows number one and provides strength. The paddler in seat four matches his cadence with number two, also providing power. The job of paddlers two and four is to make sure the canoe doesn't flip if the ama starts to rise off the water. The paddler in seat five also provides stability and strength. The steersman watches behind the canoe for swells that the canoe can ride to conserve energy. He also directs the craft toward its desired destination.

Each paddler must operate in sync with the others, fulfilling his specific duties in complete unity. If the paddlers in seats three and four pull their blades through the water too hard, the canoe will pull downward instead of forward, slowing the craft. The skill of each paddler must be honed to perfection so that all blades sink an equal depth into the water with the same extension and motion. Proper form is essential to success.

· LIFE IN MOTION ·

As you step off your safe and comfortable shore and enter the deep of your future, balance is vital. When one key area of your life is weak, the other areas will feel the stress. You may have to paddle frantically to make even the slightest progress, expending all of your energy in the first few minutes of the race. However, when each seat in your life is in proper balance with the others, you will slice through even the roughest of water. When the swells are over your head, you will ride them, allowing them to work *for* you instead of being overcome by them. This skillful living is what separates those who fail from those who succeed.

The most successful and balanced team effortlessly navigates the same swells that overwhelm less-experienced canoeists. This skill cannot be developed on the shore. There are lessons in the deep that can be found nowhere else.

> There are lessons in the deep
> that can be found nowhere else.

I've met many gifted individuals who started their race with grand hopes of victory, only to be cut short. These people are filled with grand expectations and seem to navigate their lives and achieve excellence effortlessly. They live day to day, believing that they will somehow magically end up in a happy place later in life. But they make careless decisions, doing whatever feels good, reacting to each obstacle and difficulty in a way that brings immediate pleasure. This can be a painful experience when the reality of life strikes back. Not all roads and decisions lead to a happy place.

Good intentions simply aren't enough. As a teenager, I dreamed of the relationship I would one day have with my future wife. I thought of how I would treat her, what I would buy her, where I would travel with her. When I met her, I began expressing that love to her. I had the best intentions for her joy and fulfillment and our relationship. Many years into our marriage, I realized that my intentions were meaningless if they weren't coupled with healthy choices and clear communication. Unhealthy habits and a lack of personal growth polluted the love I have for her, causing me to hurt the one I loved. I never for a nanosecond intended to cause her pain, but my lack of forward progress early in our relationship caused those intentions to be silenced by hurtful moments and memories. When it comes to relationships, preparation and skill development are essential for fulfilling our purpose.

Your generation desperately needs you and the seed of purpose that is packaged inside you. You will feel complete beyond your wildest imagination when you step into the purpose you were created for. As you allow life to shape you, as you hone skills that are foundational to success, you will rise to a level of greatness that may surprise you.

· INTO THE DEEP ·

The journey into the deep is just that: a journey. The fulfillment of our purpose is more a process than a destination. This journey is filled with more unknown variables than known ones. None of us can accurately predict all aspects of our future. In fact, many experts believe that one-fifth of all jobs that we will fill in the next five to ten years haven't even been created yet.[1]

Since our journey toward the excellence God created us for is a process, we need to be prepared for scenarios we are likely to encounter.

1. Predictable Outcomes

In some stages of life, the outcome is relatively predictable; certain actions have produced certain consequences for generations. These are unlikely to change for you and me. If you study for your midterm exam, you are likely to do better than if you don't. If you start saving money when you're young, later in life you will reap the benefits.

Recently I watched a young man, barely in his midthirties, step behind a podium to speak. He began to describe the experiences of his life. He recounted how he had married an incredible woman, owned 150 apartments, and had the quintessential Ferrari before he turned thirty. But then he dropped this bomb: "After having lost everything, including two marriages, there are some lessons that I've learned."

He had known success, but the predictable outcome of some of his choices eventually caught up with him.

2. Positive Results

Those of us who are optimistic about our futures envision managing our potential with grace and success. We anticipate experiencing the desired goal of our journey. We believe we will experience positive results from applying our specific talents.

No matter which scenarios we encounter
on our journey, they all shape us.

No matter which scenarios we encounter on our journey, they all shape us. Whether they shape us for the better or worse is up to us. We need to equip ourselves with the positive attitude of perseverance to reach our destination. Struggle is not a bad thing if it results in something positive.

3. Potential Hazards

The roadway to the ideal is often filled with hidden variables or potential hazards. These are the seemingly overpowering waves that threaten our success. These are the failures and struggles that threaten to end our journey. How we prepare for potential hazards is crucial. Knowing ahead of time that we will face difficulty—so that we can respond with the proper skills—makes all the difference in our success or failure.

4. Perspective

As we move into our future, we have a decision to make: we can either enter the future looking behind or looking ahead. Those who look only behind have little positive input about how to navigate the challenges that arise. However, if we take what we've learned from the past and then focus our attention ahead, we will develop the navigation skills to "survive and thrive" on what the horizon fails to reveal.

Looking ahead also helps us avoid adverse circumstances. When we know our makeup, we can quickly adapt for unexpected scenarios. By looking ahead, we are also able to control things that may seem uncontrollable. With our eyes on the horizon, no matter how bleak the picture may seem, we can see that what is happening to us is part of a purpose greater than anything we can comprehend. Seeing beyond the large swells and crashing waves is the difference between a terrifying experience and an exhilarating one.

· FORGED IDENTITY ·

Everything about the ocean canoe is designed with the rough journey in mind. Its design is perfected in the waters it was created to navigate. True identities are forged in the deep as well. When we are equipped with a can-do attitude and the discipline to do what is right and productive, we can embrace any obstacle with purpose. When we view our current surroundings as vital to our purpose, they take on new meaning.

We must pay attention to what God has already revealed to us about our purpose. Which people, events, activities, and dreams evoke the strongest response in us? We need to understand our capabilities and what it looks like to maintain balance in life. This understanding is essential to developing the potential locked inside. Like a new car on the showroom floor, we first need to be forged out of steel—heated, bent, and assembled—before we become a thing of beauty. Circumstances in our lives can do just that if we let them. They will take what God imagined in the design studio and bring it into reality.

Jump In

1. Have you ever felt overly prepared for something after you compared yourself to the people around you? What might remind you to keep your eye on the true standard next time?

_____

_____

_____

2. Do you feel God has revealed enough of your purpose to you for you to begin investing in it? How have you already done that?

_____

_____

_____

3. "There are lessons in the deep that can be found nowhere else." Have you found this to be true? Write something you've learned about balance from facing a challenging circumstance.

_____

_____

_____

4. The next time you face big waves, what are three ways you can retain the right perspective?

_____

_____

_____

_____

_____

_____

WELCOME TO THE DEEP

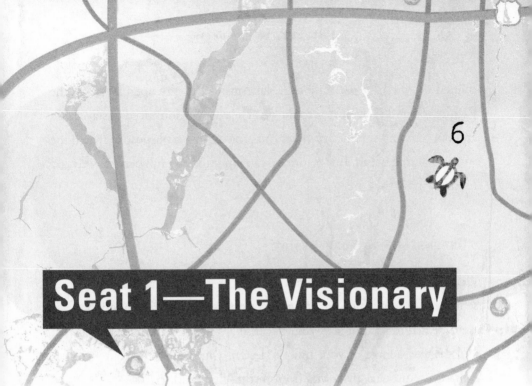

6

Seat 1—The Visionary

I n seat one are our gifts. We each have them—customized abilities to help us fulfill our purpose. They forge our unique niche in a complex world. If our life's purpose answers the "why," our gifts answer the "how." When honed, our gifts produce excellence that arises from our uniqueness.

Some species of fish grow to a certain size and then stop growing according to the size of their tank. Those who stay small are like paddlers trained to row in a perfectly calm lake instead of the open water of the Pacific. You and I have access to the open ocean. We don't need to stay small, and our gifts and unique attributes can grow us into a purpose to match the vastness of that ocean. But before we can tap into their full benefit, we need to know what they are.

• UNDERSTANDING YOUR DESIGN •

Picture a round target with a bull's-eye in the center. That bull's-eye represents exactly how you were created (your gifts and abilities) and what you were created to accomplish (your purpose). When you understand yourself and make the most of your unique design, you can hit the center of that bull's-eye. Authenticity comes from hitting that mark.

Discovering our unique attributes can be difficult, especially since we are pummeled by messages telling us we don't measure up. The average television watcher sees nearly sixteen hundred commercial images each day.[2] Do you have body odor? Buy this deodorant and all will be solved. Do you have a problem making friends? Just drink this beer or soda pop and friends will suddenly appear on your doorstep. Images scream that we need certain products and a certain lifestyle to rise to *adequacy*. But from deep within, the quiet voice of our purpose reminds us that we were not created to be adequate but *exceptional*.

A common myth says that God doesn't approve of us following dreams. I'm not talking about self-serving dreams but those dreams where we do great things, those dreams where we make a difference in our world. The Bible tells us people were was made in God's image. Does that mean that God is physically like you and me? No. God is a spirit. God made us in

His image on the inside more than the outside. We, like God, have the ability to imagine. Why would God have created us to imagine great things only to squelch that with practicality? The pursuit of our God-given dreams and the use of our gifts toward that end help us to become the people God created us to be. God gave us a powerful imagination. Those dreams He sets before us point us toward our purpose. When we act on those dreams planted inside of us, we acknowledge their divine source and bring glory to God.

There is a myth that says
God doesn't approve of us following dreams.

Missing the bull's-eye, even by a small margin, produces negative results. If we are designed to be a round peg, then in order to hit that bull's-eye, we need to fit into that round hole God has prepared for us. We need to discover and acknowledge our roundness and slip into our place. But sometimes we notice a square hole that looks enticing. We think, "Oh, how I wish I could fit in the square hole. Life would be incredible if I could be in that square hole." We spend entire seasons of life trying to cram ourselves into a hole that we were not designed for. In doing so, we lose our authenticity.

If you have ever tried to work at a job that didn't match your gifts, you understand what I am talking about. Let's say you're a people person—you love that face-to-face interaction. If you have a cubicle job in front of a computer, you're going to feel like an imposter. Maybe you are a detail-oriented person who is introverted and doesn't like large groups of people.

A job involving public speaking would be terrifying to you. When we're round pegs trying to fit into square holes, we spend far too much energy merely trying to survive. But when a round peg finds its round hole, that energy can be channeled into deeper creativity.

· GOOD NEWS ABOUT YOUR GIFTS ·

Your gifts were placed inside you by God. You were meticulously planned out from the beginning of time. The psalmist wrote:

> For you created my inmost being;
>> you knit me together in my mother's womb.
> I praise you because I am fearfully and wonderfully made;
>> your works are wonderful,
>> I know that full well.
> My frame was not hidden from you
>> when I was made in the secret place.
> When I was woven together in the depths of the earth,
>> your eyes saw my unformed body.
> All the days ordained for me
>> were written in your book
>> before one of them came to be. (Psalm 139:13–16)

God gives us everything we need to *begin* our race, but we don't have everything we'll need to *finish* our race when we start. We need to gain wisdom along the way to be a great husband or wife. We need to develop our skills to become a successful CEO or student.

God isn't a bit surprised by your abilities or destiny. He's not waiting for you to be someone you aren't. He loves it when you use the gifts and abilities He's given you. You'll make the greatest impact in life in the area of your giftedness. It is our gifts that will bring us into circles of great influence and relationships. God knew that before you were ever born.

True fulfillment will only come when a gift
is used according to the Creator's wishes.

Our gifts are also for the common good. They aren't for our personal gain or to make us look important. They're designed to serve a greater purpose. Remember, anything not used for its intended purpose is subject to misuse or abuse. This is especially true for our gifts or abilities. I know eloquent speakers who communicate with grace and skill. Some of them use their ability for their own gain. True fulfillment will only come when a gift is used according to the Creator's wishes.

Remember, you have everything you need to do what God wants you to do. The Bible says, "His divine power has given us everything we need for life and godliness through our knowledge of him who called us by his own glory and goodness" (2 Peter 1:3). That's right. God didn't design us to be able to fulfill our purposes independent of one another. We are only complete in the body of Christ. You may have the gift of being able to stand in front of hundreds of people and speak. That's great. You may have creativity seeping from your pores. Or maybe you're great with numbers—you'd make a terrific accountant—but would never stand in front of a room of people. Maybe that leads you to question, "What in the world can I do with my gift?

I'm just an accountant." Let me ask you this: Where would churches be without accountants? Where would servants be without planners? Where would faithful workers be without creative ideas to follow? When believers use their gifts in concert with one another, the result is a symphony that moves the hearts and minds of people according to God's purposes.

As a general rule, I think we should invest about 80 percent of our time perfecting what we consider our greatest strengths and the rest of the time learning new things or working on the weaker areas of our lives. If we focus too much of our attention on our weaknesses, we can lose focus and miss the bull's-eye.

> If we focus too much of our attention on our weaknesses, we can lose focus and miss the bull's-eye.

Even though we may have been given wonderful gifts and the ability to perfect them, God's plan for us still requires His participation. Fulfilling His great purpose for you will require His power and, at times, miraculous intervention. God is strong in our weaknesses. Some of the most historic, world-changing moments in Scripture came about when people admitted their inadequacy and cried out for God's help. God can make fearful people the strongest warriors.

• DISCOVERING YOUR GIFTS •

The first seat in our canoe sets the pace. As we step into the deep, three things will help us pursue our purpose.

1. Past Experiences

Take an inventory of your life experiences. Some experiences help you discover your gifts and articulate your purpose. God knows the history of your life. Ask these questions when conducting your inventory:

What excites you? What you love is a big clue to the gifts you possess. Answer this question: "If every job on earth paid the same wage, what would you love to do?" Love is a powerful gift-shaper, because love gives birth to wisdom. We have the ability to gain a deep understanding about things we deeply enjoy.

What do you love to talk about? Certain areas of interest make even the most introverted person talkative. What are those areas for you? Your gifts are revealed in the day-to-day routines of life.

What has brought you the deepest satisfaction? Write down ten things that bring you deep satisfaction or joy. A good friend of mine recalled a picture he drew in the third grade. This crayon-wielding Picasso drew a picture of himself driving a cargo truck. But this wasn't just any cargo truck. It was one filled with tiny black crayon circles, representing hundreds of filmstrips. (Before the advent of DVDs and the Internet, students watched strips of film through a projector. One lucky student was chosen to manually advance the strip when a tone on the cassette tape—or record—sounded. Pretty high-tech, don't you think?) This man is a college professor today. Even as a young child, he was gaining satisfaction from demonstrating his love for teaching. His teaching gift appeared in grade school, and today he shapes the hearts and minds of a young generation.

What do those who know you best expect from you? Many times parents, teachers, coaches, pastors, and others close to you will recognize qualities you can't see, attributes like leadership and teachability.

2. Areas of Interest

What are the things you really enjoy studying? What organizations do you participate in with enthusiasm? What could you teach others to do? These areas of interest probably utilize some of your greatest gifts.

3. Wise Counsel

One of the best things you can do is talk with people who do what you would like to do. I recommend asking them these questions:

- What is your story?
- What helped make you successful?
- If you had to do it over again, what would you do differently?
- What advice would you give someone coming into the field today?
- Who are a few key leaders in this field?
- What are "must read" books for anyone in this field?
- What would you consider essential principles for success in this field?
- What is your next goal, and how do you plan to accomplish it?
- How does your planning process work?
- What obstacles should I look out for?

The Bible tells us that our gifts are more effective when we walk with the wise (see Proverbs 13:20). Consider a future great musician. She may first take lessons in school. Then one day a master musician hears her play and offers private lessons. She spends years in one-on-one training with one of the best. She becomes an accomplished musician herself and then can mentor others. This process is also true for other areas of life. For example, if you want to become a great husband some day, spend time around a great husband and allow him to share about his life and how he relates to his wife. Then you could become a much better husband.

· PRACTICE PERFECTION ·

King David led with "integrity of heart" and "skillful hands" (Psalm 78:72). No doubt he was equipped with certain skills, perfected in his youth, which he used later to accomplish his purpose. During our youth and young adult years, we have the opportunity to hone and perfect our gifts. But it is also a responsibility. Nobody can hone our skills for us; it requires an investment of time.

Time is the earth's currency.

Time is the earth's currency. God gives us time, and we are invited to invest it. When we invest it in people, we develop friendships. When we invest in our education and work ethic, we earn intelligence and money. When we invest in mentors or teachers who can help shape us, we reap excellence. The greater the level of excellence we achieve with our gifts, the greater the impact those gifts will have in fulfilling God's purpose for us. If we don't intentionally invest our time in our strengths, gifts, and ideas, we will end up mediocre in many areas of life.

· PROPER APPLICATION ·

A job is something we do that brings us money. A vocation is something more—something greater than mere employment. A vocation is a calling. It is something that compels us toward our divine purpose. It may or may not sustain our livelihood, but it's a place where our gifts and purpose meet, carving out our unique place in this world. And when our passions and areas of strength meet a deep need in others, we know we are on the right track.

As you pursue your assignment from God, you will encounter channels where navigation is difficult. Pound the water with your paddle and scan the horizon for buoys marking your progress. Even when the work is difficult or seems mundane and meaningless, you may still be drawing nearer to the next buoy. Trust the stability you've acquired, and lock into the course that brings you closer to fulfilling God's purpose.

JUMP IN

1. Use your imagination. What is the most incredible thing you can imagine yourself accomplishing?

_____

_____

_____

_____

2. Knowing that you will not have at the start what you will need to finish your journey, what skills do you want to gain and master?

_____

_____

_____

_____

How can you be a lifelong learner in these areas?

_____

_____

_____

_____

3. We each only have twenty-four hours in a day. If each hour were a golden boxcar, what would you fill them with? Spend time strategically planning your daily routine.

_____

_____

_____

_____

7

Seat 2—The Balancer

S eat two is about strength. On the way to our next navigational marker, the occupant of seat two serves two vital roles. First, seat two sets the pace for seat four while matching his paddling rhythm with the person in seat one. Seat two must know seat one's patterns well enough that he can remain in sync without even watching. Seasoned paddle teams occasionally practice blindfolded in order to learn the feel of proper paddling.

That's not all seat two is responsible for. When the ama slaps the water, that means the canoe is rocking and must be steadied. Seat two has the job of judging whether the slap is normal or a sign of an impending flip. If a veteran paddler feels the canoe might overturn, he dives to the left, throwing his weight onto the ama to keep the canoe from capsizing.

On the journey to your purpose, your attitude is seat two. Attitude is a significant contributor to success. No matter how gifted you are, attitude has the power to slow or speed your journey. Though organizations, corporations, and other groups look closely at your gifts, your attitude is what often tips the scale and gets you that job or earns you that position on the committee. Gifts may earn you awards, scholarships, and other triumphs, but it's your attitude that often determines whether you stay on top. Can you maintain balance to survive adversity and remain humble?

· WHAT IS ATTITUDE? ·

If you're like many young adults, you probably put a fair amount of thought or consideration into what you choose to wear. And if a job interview or date is somehow involved, the amount of thought increases considerably. But of all the things we wear, our attitude is the most important.

We wear our attitude each and every day. Our attitude is essentially our outward behavior expressing inward feelings. It's driven by our habits of thought. Someone has said that life is 10 percent what happens to us and 90 percent how we respond to it. During times of stress and testing, our character is shaped and subsequently revealed through our attitude. All of life's ups and downs come face to face with our attitude and are turned into either something productive or something destructive.

In Hawaii it is customary to honor people by giving them leis, which are made with many combinations of flowers and fragrances. Pikake and white ginger are two of the most exotic scents I have encountered. If you meet someone wearing one of these leis, you will be amazed by how incredible they smell.

> Of all the things we wear,
> our attitude is the most important.

Our attitude is like a lei. We wear what we have chosen to string together from our internal garden of thoughts. We can choose the beautiful aroma of exotic Polynesian flowers or the pungent odor of a wet dog. As we interact with one another, we spread the odor of our lei—good or bad.[3]

An attitude can attract people or repel them. It can strengthen relationships at crucial moments or destroy them. It can bring healing or death. In some ways, your attitude is the determining factor that will dictate whether you succeed or fail. It is often more important than skills, gifts, or resources. Here's why: your expectations and approach to life are the result of your attitude.

Your attitude is often revealed by the answer to this simple question: How is your world treating you? If you feel your world is treating you well, your attitude is probably positive. If you believe those around you are treating you poorly, you may conclude that the world is against you—determined to give you a lifetime of struggle and hardship.

A positive attitude can limit the effects of wrongdoing, make the most of a missed opportunity, and turn something painful into something positive.

Those around you will go on with their lives regardless of your attitude, but you will be greatly impacted by it. What you sow in attitude, you will reap (Galatians 6:7).

You can't control much of what happens to you, but you can control how it affects and shapes you. You didn't choose your parents or control the environment that has molded you. Your past decisions can't be changed. People who wronged you or violated your trust committed an atrocity, but you can't erase these scenarios. What you can do is customize your attitude to make the most of each of these situations, just like the apostle Paul, who wrote in Philippians that he had "learned the secret of being content in any and every situation" (Philippians 4:12).

A good attitude is not something we receive at the moment of salvation but is something we develop during our journey. A positive attitude is one of the most powerful forces in our daily paddling and navigating toward our purpose.

• THE POWER OF CHOICE •

When the person in seat two is an experienced paddler, race-saving adjustments are made quickly, even before others detect trouble. How many times have you overreacted and caused more damage than the original incident would have? Maybe you carried an offense too long and that caused you to fly off the handle and cause hurt. An attitude that is always ready to respond *correctly* can change the momentum of a questionable or even disastrous scenario.

One of the benefits of our attitude is that it helps us to control uncontrollable events. It's a common myth that all successful people just had better advantages, resources, or luck than less successful people. The truth is, many successful people have faced more setbacks than you or I have—they just saw these as steppingstones or opportunities to learn and improve. A good attitude serves as a solid foundation for success and achieving our God-given purpose.

It's a myth that successful people had better resources or advantages than less successful people.

Jesus stressed the importance of attitude when early in His ministry He taught His followers the Beatitudes (Matthew 5:1–12). He presented these attitude-shaping concepts before teaching other more advanced topics.

A positive and confident attitude keeps the canoe stable in rough water. When the ama slaps the water and danger lurks, a positive attitude responds and keeps the canoe from overturning. No matter what circumstances are crashing around us, our attitude can keep us afloat and making forward progress.

Conditions are constantly changing, but a good attitude can help us quickly and efficiently deal with whatever comes our way.

• PICK YOUR GRADE •

Imagine the first day of your most difficult class. Wouldn't it be great if your professor asked the students to come to his desk and simply pick the grade they want? A to F, your choice. That's exactly what God has done for us. In Deuteronomy we read that God gave His people the ability to choose for themselves how their lives would end: "I have set before you life and death, blessings and curses. Now choose life" (Deuteronomy 30:19). The choice is ours. It is not favorable circumstances or luck that make us successful. It's not that "big break" that never seems to come. It's the attitude we develop. Remember, our adventure into the deep isn't only about the destination but also the journey itself. A positive attitude will increase the reward along the way.

· CULTIVATING POSITIVE ATTITUDE ·

We have a choice. We can either master our attitude or become a victim of it. Choices we made yesterday have shaped who we are today. And the choices we make today will forge our tomorrows. Our future depends on the ability to cultivate a positive attitude, which can exponentially increase the effectiveness of our gifts. A great attitude can help you achieve your purpose with few regrets. A bad attitude can be the force that stops you in your tracks. On the unpredictable waters of life, the core quality of a good attitude is more valuable than favorable conditions.

When cultivating a positive attitude, we must first be convinced that we can do it. We can't control everything in our lives, but we can cultivate a good attitude. And if we don't have one naturally or we've developed a poor one because of bad habits—there is hope. We can change. The Bible says we are "being transformed into his likeness with ever-increasing glory, which comes from the Lord, who is the Spirit" (2 Corinthians 3:18). When we work at developing a positive attitude, we are cooperating with the Spirit of God. He is at work in us, constantly refining us. For His work to take place, we must allow Him to remove those thoughts and trained responses that critically damage our attitude.

I absolutely love Jeeps. I love checking out the latest models, as well as seeing concept vehicles and looking at all the modifications Jeep owners make. I dream of taking my new Jeep Rubicon onto the beach, with its thirty-three-inch BFGoodrich Mud-Terrain tires conquering the sand with ease. I imagine the top down, waves crashing in the distance, my wife and kids strapped in, enjoying the ride. You get the picture. My fixation with these vehicles has done something to the way I see the world around me. I notice every Jeep that passes me, even on the interstate at 75 miles per hour. I have unintentionally trained my eyes to notice Jeeps.

When we work at developing a positive attitude,
we are cooperating with the Spirit of God.

Each day our attitude takes our attention into the gym of our daily thoughts and trains it. There we determine what we're looking for. Our attention then feeds our attitude, and the cycle repeats. As you can imagine, this concept can work for us or against us. When we look for the best in people, we find the most amazing people in the world. And they're *everywhere*. If we expect negative results, we discover them in every circumstance. Some of us are conditioned because of past relationships to expect rejection. Guess what that does to our attitude? When we experience things in life that we don't understand, we need to use our attitude to train our eyes to look for signs of God's hand and presence. As my mentor, Wayne Cordeiro, mentions in his book *Attitudes That Attract Success,* "train your eyes to see the evidence of His presence, not His absence."[4]

The refocusing of our eyes often requires us to see things from a different perspective. The Father is aware of everything that happens in our life. He sees our purpose and knows it has much greater value than our time on earth. Remember, our life is just a grain of sand. When we step back and view things from God's perspective, we can see the value of maintaining a good attitude. We can see the bigger picture of how we are shaped and how we shape others. And we can enjoy the many "silver linings" God has created in our lives.

Practice really does make perfect. Considering our potential and how attitude affects it, every struggle we face adds value. And as we act on what we know is right, a good attitude will eventually become more natural.

In the few years you've been alive, you may have developed an attitude that has flooded your canoe. Weighed down with past regrets, hurts, and pains, your paddlers struggle to make progress. The writer of Hebrews tells us to "strip off every weight that slows us down" (Hebrews 12:1, NLT). Wrong attitudes have a tendency to do just that—weigh us down. We need to bail out the water to lighten the boat so we can paddle through the rough water.

· QUESTIONS THAT DEMAND ANSWERS ·

In order to cultivate a more positive attitude, we must take a look at our *current* attitude. We need to examine circumstances that make us feel bad and take action to improve.

- What circumstances bring you down emotionally? Why?
- What thoughts are you meditating on? Do they bring you up or down? Do they make your canoe lighter or heavier? Are they productive or destructive?

- What does the Bible say about these matters? Remember, the Bible is what helps you refocus and keep the canoe skimming the waves.
- What must you do to change? How will you master the weaker areas of your emotions and no longer be a victim?
- What's your master plan to improve your attitude?

· AGENTS OF CHANGE ·

Our attitudes include habits of thought and ways of viewing life we have been developing since birth. An attitude begins with a single thought. When we meditate on that thought, it influences our choices. Choices we repeat become habits. Habits of thinking are attitudes. They become nearly instinctual.

Let's examine how this process can work in a negative way. If you meditate on a negative thought, that will eventually produce a negative choice. That negative choice will produce a wrong action. And when repeated, that wrong action will reinforce a negative attitude.

If we are serious about mastering our attitude, then we need to examine what causes our habits of thought. John Maxwell, in his book *The Winning Attitude,* gives these eight steps for changing bad habits into good ones. These can easily be adapted to help us adjust our attitude.

1. List your bad habits.
2. What was the original cause?
3. What are the supporting causes?
4. Determine a positive habit to replace the bad one.
5. Think about the good habit, its benefits and results.
6. Take action to develop this habit.

7. Daily act upon this habit for reinforcement.

8. Reward yourself by noting one of the benefits from your good habit.[5]

· MAINTAINING A POSITIVE ATTITUDE ·

A positive attitude doesn't usually come as standard equipment. It is usually an optional feature that we must choose as we attempt to navigate well toward our purpose. But whether it's standard or optional equipment, a positive attitude requires daily maintenance. Like other character traits, the motivation for cultivating and maintaining a positive attitude comes from within.

Positive attitudes don't make the rough waters less violent. When we come upon those rough waters and see that they're not suddenly calmed by our attitude, we may be tempted to scrap the positive attitude altogether. But these are the sorts of moments when we most need to win.

Life's waves can either make us bitter or better.

Life's waves can either make us bitter or better. What happens *in* us is far more important than what happens *to* us. We can't allow negative circumstances, hurtful words from others, and other external circumstances to control our choices. James tells us to consider it a gift when we face tests and challenges. Why? Because "under pressure, your faith-life is forced into the open and shows its true colors. So don't try to get out of anything prematurely. Let it do its work so you become mature and well-developed, not deficient in any way" (James 1:2–4, MSG). We become better when we allow these external issues to force us to respond with a positive attitude.

I think it's important to remember that not all of our journey will be through rough water. Seasons of ease and difficulty will come and go. We'll face plenty of big decisions in the calm water, but usually that calm will give us the time and wisdom to choose wisely. Most wrong choices are made during rough water, because we tend to let external forces control our thinking. When we make big decisions during the calm seasons, we remove the rough water's power to bring us down.

• KODAK MOMENTS •

Our attitude constantly feeds itself by taking pictures and storing them away for later reinforcement. These are pictures of past experiences taken through the lens of our perception. Two photographers can take pictures of the same event with completely different results. Many of us have mental iPhoto libraries filled with painful experiences: "This is my mom and dad fighting." "Oh, I remember this one; this is when my mom moved us out and divorced my dad." "This is when my friends humiliated me." "This one is one of my favorites—when I failed to make the team for the third year in a row."

Allow me to introduce you to Mr. Delete Key. It's time to begin replacing our negative memories with positive ones taken during seasons of joy: "This is when my wife and I were teenagers serving together in our youth group." "I'll never forget when he first told me he loved me." "He has such a funny laugh." "Mom used to bake with me every Christmas." "That picture I painted in class was incredible." These are the pictures we need to capture in our memories to cultivate a more positive attitude. During the seasons of joy, we need to snap lots of these pictures. One day you might wake up and discover your marriage has hit rough waters. A positive attitude doesn't grab for the camera to record all of the pain and mistakes; it picks up the iPhoto and begins scrolling through the joyful moments of your relationship. It reinforces the decision you made in the calm waters to spend the rest of your lives together. Your attitude throws its weight on the ama, and keeps the canoe from flipping.

Good memories are that important.

• RIDE THE WAVES •

Seasoned paddlers pray for rough water! On flat water, paddlers sweat for each inch of forward progress. Their paddles' blades are all that propel their canoe. However, when the swells pick up and the waves form, paddlers can arrive at their destination quicker by being carried forward not only by their paddles but also by the power in the water.

We are guaranteed to encounter
rough water on our journey.

We are guaranteed to encounter rough water on our journey. It can be scary and threaten the stability of our canoe. But it can also increase our efficiency and forward progress. Even though training happens in the harbor, it is the open sea that provides the best life lessons. When we run into the rough water, our attitude can make or break the journey.

JUMP IN

1. What areas in your life can you not control that you wish you could?

How can your attitude toward those areas be improved?

2. Do you feel that you are a master or a victim of your attitude? What are two ways you can better manage your attitude?

3. Does the camera of your mind capture negative or positive images more easily? List the most vivid images in your iPhoto memory library.

_____

_____

_____

_____

_____

_____

Memories are nurtured. We can either nurture the positive ones that bring us pleasure and make us laugh, or we can nurture the negative ones that rehash the hurt we've experienced. Label each of the above memories as positive or negative. Then write "delete" next to the negative ones as you pray about them, asking God to forgive the people who caused them and to take the hurt away.

For further study, check out these resources:

- *Attitudes That Attract Success* by Wayne Cordeiro
- *The Winning Attitude: Your Keys to Personal Success* by John C. Maxwell

8

Seat 3—
The Power Position

S eat three provides balance. The person in the canoe's third seat must keep the canoe steady while providing power. Unlike seat two, seat three isn't expected to adjust the balance. This seat doesn't set the pace or lead the way, but it is absolutely vital to successful navigation.

Hawaiian canoes are quite stable in the water. Actually, I should qualify that. They are quite stable in *calm* water. Seasoned crews learn to balance the canoe with their bodies in rough water. To maintain balance and stability, paddlers must paddle on different sides of the canoe. This concept was demonstrated during one of our church's Pastors Practicums.

Church leaders from all over the world came together in Honolulu to learn how to develop and enhance their ministries. A highlight of the week was when the pastors were given the opportunity to paddle canoes as teams. During one of the friendly competitions, one team got confused about how to maintain balance. Their haphazard paddling led to an upside-down canoe and six wet pastors—even in the calm waters of the bay.

No matter how strong our gifts and how good our attitude, we can flip our canoe in the calmest of waters if we don't maintain balance. God knows how stable our canoe is. He knows what waters we are prepared to navigate and what will flip us. Sometimes He allows us to experience things that take us in over our head. Other times He holds us back. He always knows best.

> It's during testing that we often
> see the places in our lives that aren't
> ready for the journey's next leg.

Sometimes when we experience success, we start to believe that makes us stable enough for the long haul. We become satisfied with our career, the promotion we just earned, or the relationships we've developed, and we think we've "made it." But the level of stability we have today will not be enough to get us to the next navigational buoy.

God may test us during these seasons. It's during this testing that we often see the places in our lives that aren't ready for the journey's next leg. Like the paddler in seat number three, we learn at this point what it takes to provide stability. This is when we grow to understand how to maintain balance.

· DON'T ROCK YOUR BOAT ·

Successful people make thousands of small, right decisions. They are not always the most gifted, eloquent, or charismatic people, but they are people who have learned from their mistakes and adjusted accordingly. They take calculated risks when risk is required. They are well rounded, having gained a level of mastery in core life areas that bring stability.

> Successful people make
> thousands of small, right decisions.

I have heard many leaders say, "My plate is too full." It's true. Their lives are filled to capacity with all they can handle. One of the benefits of tests, trials, and other seasons of preparation designed by God is that these give us a larger plate. If you've lifted weights, you understand this concept. A personal trainer's job isn't to lighten the weight to something you can easily manage. Taking the weight off the bar will not make better lifters. Instead, the trainer strategically selects the weight that will strain your muscles to grow.

Seat number three supplies the strength to match any circumstance.

· STRENGTH TRAINING ·

I believe there are seven areas of our life that are "must wins." We need to train in all seven if we expect to handle increasingly rougher waters. If we are deficient in any one of these areas, the other six will feel the stress.[6]

Must Win #1: Faith

Understanding the heart of God and developing a relationship with Him is the first step toward a life of meaning and true success. Everything else, no matter how rewarding, will fall short without well-developed faith.

When we view our lives through an understanding of eternity and God's ultimate plan, we can major on the major areas of our lives and minor on the minors. When we do this, seeking temporary pleasure isn't quite as important as it used to be.

God desires for each of us to know Him. The plans He has for us require His involvement. The journey into the deep is about His plan, not ours. Moses, Joshua, Caleb, and David cooperated with God's plan. They were a part of something much greater. When our faith life is out of whack, we seek to adjust the other areas to compensate for the gaping hole. Yet nothing and nobody can fill that void except for God.

Must Win #2: Healthy Life

I once asked a seasoned paddler for advice about purchasing a canoe. "Which brands are the best?" I asked. He listed a dozen canoe manufacturers, identifying each model's strengths and weaknesses. "That one is good because it's heavy and stable. This one's good because it's strong and can take a heavy pounding from coral, rocks, and waves." Pausing for a second, he looked up at me and said, "The type of canoe isn't as important as the engine."

It took me a moment to catch what he was saying, but he was absolutely right. A skilled paddler can make any piece of fiberglass skim the water. Just like that paddler, the physical body is the engine that propels our journey. When the engine stalls, the journey stalls.

We decide what our health and appearance will be and must develop healthy habits to support achieving our purpose. How many great men and women paddle into the deep and experience health setbacks from choices made earlier in life? Physical exercise increases blood flow and brain activity. It also unleashes creativity. When we are weak in this area of balance, we become tired, run-down, and unable to fulfill those things our heart desires. It's been said that in this generation, the quality of our health will not depend on what medical science can do for us, but rather on what medical science can convince us to do for ourselves. A healthy lifestyle can make all the difference in our journey.

Must Win #3: Self-Development

We must be lifelong students. A portion of our time should be invested in education, knowledge, and self-improvement. For example, before you get engaged, study great marriages. Read marriage books. Surround yourself with people who have strong families. Learn, learn, learn.

Change seems to be the only constant in our world. So, to successfully navigate the future, you need to be a continuous learner. Take advantage of your time. Download an audio book or podcast of a great leader's teaching and listen in the car. Read one self-improvement book each month. Don't allow yourself to become intellectually stagnant. The day you stop learning is the day you admit you'll never get any smarter. Think you have mastery over technology? In a decade, eighth graders will leave middle school with more knowledge than you now have.

We need to ride the wave of knowledge to stay sharp and effective.

Must Win #4: Social Life

Healthy friendships, community involvement, and involvement in a local church are vital to the proper discovery of gifts and to social development. We were not designed to do life alone; we were built for relationships. Relationships reflect a life changed by following Christ. Jesus was asked to sum up all the good stuff taught in the Bible. "It's a big book, so give us the Cliffs Notes. What's the most important thing in here?" Jesus contemplated and gave this answer: " 'Love the Lord your God with all your heart and with all your soul and with all your mind.' This is the first and greatest commandment. And the second is like it: 'Love your neighbor as yourself.' All the Law and the Prophets hang on these two commandments" (Matthew 22:37–40).

Loving our neighbors—this happens in our social life. Maybe it means forgiving those who have hurt you. Or maybe it means mentoring someone who needs a leader. There are a million ways that love plays out in relationships. So how important is your social life? Well, it's one of the Big Two, according to Jesus. Sounds pretty important to me.

Your social life can be one of the most rewarding aspects of the journey.

Must Win #5: Finances

What we do with our money when we're young impacts the long road ahead. Right decisions now will make the difference years later. A clear plan is vital, and the earlier we can set that plan, the better. We must escape the common financial mind-set in our culture of "buy now, pay later." We need to be realistic about our money and work toward the goal of only buying what we can pay for now. As we begin to move beyond compulsion and credit, we take control of our financial future. The earlier we discover how to do this, the better. And there is often no better way to learn this than from a seasoned mentor who can advise you on how to master your money. If you feel this is an area you need to focus on, consider who you know who might help you.

Strong goals, smart planning, and discipline will make finances a balancing factor for the journey.

Must Win #6: Family

Few people influence us as much as those who raised us, so as adults we need to deal with any negative issues from our past while developing positive habits for the future. Many of us have painful memories from our family of origin. We need to understand these hurts and ask Jesus to heal them. We need to establish and uphold healthy boundaries between our family of origin and the family we create.

Good relationships just don't happen. They require work. Both husband and wife need to be lifelong learners as well as willing and able to identify those areas within themselves that may need improvement. Ephesians 5:21–33 talks about submission to each other in marriage. The submission of the wife to her husband is discussed in three verses. The husband's treatment of his wife is discussed in nine verses. (What does that say about men, I wonder.) Both partners must learn to respond quickly and lovingly to what the other needs.

Must Win #7: Vocation

Remember what I said earlier: a vocation is a calling. Our vocation ought to reflect the life we are striving to develop. It is usually determined by the other six "must wins." Keep in mind, this isn't about money. A high-paying career doesn't guarantee a healthy future—in fact, in some cases it can destroy a family. A slight imbalance in *any* area can cause others to wobble. Our vocation is the place where our gifts and the world's deep needs meet.

• THE SEVEN IN ACTION •

When these seven "must wins" are in balance, we achieve success in seat three. Voices in our culture tell us that *work* is the source of reward in life. Yet when a job takes more space than it should, we experience imbalance. Perhaps we spend less time with those we love. Taking care of our physical health falls into the "when I have time" category. Maybe we discontinue our education and personal development, using that time to pursue the almighty dollar instead. Ignoring the development of our faith forces the other six "must wins" to carry a weight they were not designed to carry. And we can't draw from others in our social life what we can only get from our Creator. Balance in all seven areas keeps us well rounded and produces an invisible foundation that supports our purpose.

Occasionally we may encounter an event that causes imbalance beyond our control. We lose our job or lose an important relationship. During these times it's important to pour our energy into the other six areas while we search for godly solutions and deal with the repercussions. If bad news comes, be intentional about keeping the other six areas strong.

Run an extra two miles or plug into a new small group in your church. Strengthening stable areas will keep the imbalance from throwing your entire life into a tailspin.

• Guarding Your Balance •

Emerging leaders and young adults face a variety of threats to their balance. Thankfully, we have many practical ways to improve our chances to win those "must wins."

Today, there is no shortage of things to put on our to-do lists. Even children need planners to keep track of their schedules. Unfortunately, we often live far too close to the edge. Even though our "plates" grow bigger as we face the many challenges of life, they will still have limited capacity. So one of the things we need to always carry on our plates is space to breathe. We need *margin*.

Margin is the space between the load we carry and the top limit of our carrying capacity. We have limits to the stress we carry, the busyness we experience, the time we consume, and the thoughts we manage. There is a hundred-foot drop at the end of that maximum capacity.

Margin is the space between the load we carry
and the top limit of our carrying capacity.

Some of us can comfortably maintain a life filled to 95 percent of our capacity. We're comfortable, at least until some unexpected activity pushes us over the edge—this is the proverbial straw that breaks the camel's back.

In reality, it's not the unexpected activity that is at fault but rather the fact that we didn't include enough margin to allow for it.

Here's a scenario that may sound familiar: Filled with vision and enthusiasm, you begin working at a job you love. When you see the exciting potential of a promotion on the horizon, you give more of yourself to work than a healthy balance would allow. You compromise your margin. In your attempt to impress key decision makers with your work ethic, this increased pace and workload soon become the norm. Your measure of personal value starts to come disproportionately from your busyness. Then some variable enters your life from out of nowhere, and over the edge you go.

The morning run goes out the window and is replaced by the strongest drink you can find at Starbucks. You start to snap at those you love the most because you're always stressed. You have no time to read a good book. Life begins to run *you,* and you are at the mercy of its momentum. One day you notice you've become angry and cynical—not because you're normally an angry or cynical person but because you're living a marginless life. You feel lonely too, which makes you even angrier.

The prophet Isaiah warned against a marginless life when he wrote, "Woe to those who add house to house and join field to field, until there is no more room, so that you have to live alone in the midst of the land" (Isaiah 5:8, NASB). Marginless lives fill our interior space with stuff until there is no more space left.

How, then, can we develop a life with healthy margins?

The reserve of energy that a margin provides fills a tank from which we draw rest, creativity, and other positive experiences. That tank is also drained by activities in our life—entertainment, exercise, relationships, work, classes, or other things that draw our attention. Problems and stressors drain the tank too. Not only do we need to find out what drains our tank, we need to discover what fills it.

Filling our tank builds our margin's reserve. You probably already know instinctively which relationships and activities replenish your energy, increase your creativity, and bring you joy. If the goal is to maintain margin, our fill-ups need to equal or exceed our drains.

What activities are the greatest drains in your life? What are the things, relationships, and activities that fill you up?

Although Wayne Cordeiro is an author and pastor of one of most influential churches in America, several days each week, he gets in the water and paddles around Oahu. Paddling is one of his fill-ups. The day he doesn't have time to paddle is the day he takes a step toward that hundred-foot drop. For his sake, his family's sake, and the sake of the worldwide ministry he runs, these fill-ups are essential.

If you are dating, courting, engaged, or married, sit down with your partner and separately list your drains and fill-ups. Then exchange your lists. Learn from this list what things you can do to help fill your loved one's tank regularly. You can do this with your children too. Doing this can create healthy personal margins and strengthen your relationships. By working from the source of your strength and developing healthy margins, you will be able to maintain a sustainable pace as you navigate the deep water of your purpose.

JUMP IN

1. Write one way you can improve your balance in each of the following areas:

Faith: _____

Health: _____

Self-Improvement: _____

Social Life: _____

Finances: _____

Family: _____

Vocation: _____

2. Based on the above, what three things can you start right away to gain better life balance?

_____

_____

_____

9

Seat 4—The Corrector

S eat four signifies the necessary perseverance.

All of us experience circumstances and pain that bring our progress to
a screeching halt. The ability to survive setbacks isn't something that nec-
essarily calls upon our gifts, nor is it as visible as our attitude. But the seat
of perseverance is a key position in our canoe. How we handle difficult circumstances is crucial to the success of our journey.

"Don't worry—our sharks don't bite; they just sniff. And they only like
white meat." With words like those, well-meaning Hawaiians "comfort"

those of us who are less than comfortable with the environment. Do I have to tell you that words like those are the last thing I want to hear when entering deep blue water? Comforting? I don't think so.

So there I was, in the deep water off the shore of Honolulu. In the pit of my stomach, I felt an eerie sense that something was wrong. "Hurricane Daniel," the steersman stated calmly. I knew exactly what he was talking about. Many miles away, the hurricane was producing unusual swells that we were feeling in our small watercraft.

The canoe flipped upside down and
dumped all of us into the shark-infested waters.

Slap. Slap. I heard the ama bouncing against the water. *I know that means something important.* In the middle of that thought, I felt the ama lift off the water and hang three feet off the waves. Then it happened. The canoe flipped upside down and dumped all of us into the shark-infested waters. I was shaken—floating a mile off the coast of Hawaii. We had not prepared for something like this while practicing in calm water.

Without fail, we all will experience things we're not prepared for on our journey. How we handle being dumped into shark-infested waters makes the difference between success or failure, winning or losing, quitting or finishing.

· LIFE IS NOT FAIR ·

Life is not fair. How well we are prepared for life's unfair moments is directly connected to what those moments produce in us.

We may experience financial hardships, disintegrating relationships, problems with our health, or other issues. The bottom line is that struggles come. If God eliminated struggle, He would be taking away one of the most effective ways to forge character and depth in us. God uses struggle to prepare us for "what's next" in life. We are not equipped on the shore or in the quiet of calmer waters for everything we need to find success in the deep. That equipping is forged in difficult, often painful moments.

Jesus lived a sinless life. Yet even Jesus experienced suffering. The Bible says that Jesus "learned obedience from what he suffered" (Hebrews 5:8). Like Jesus, we learn obedience—we grow in our understanding of what it means to live a life of faith—not from the suffering itself but from what we *learn* from the suffering.

· THE ROLE OF SUFFERING ·

Consider the analogy of the chick and the egg. Before a baby chick enters the great big world, it finds itself in a safe and comfortable environment. The chick's home inside the egg feels just perfect. At a critical point in its young life, the chick has an eye-opening revelation that the same shell keeping it comfortable and safe is also restricting its life. So the little chick begins pecking at the shell. As it breaks through the shell, its tenacious hard work enables it to obtain the strength and endurance to survive in a new environment. Well-meaning observers have tried to help chicks in this process by cracking the shell for them. But by short-circuiting the chicks' necessary pecking process, the helpers kill the birds instead. The hard work of breaking out of the shell is what gives a chick the strength to live outside of it.[7]

Avoidance of struggle traps us where we are; it dooms us to a stillborn sort of life. Our journey isn't just about reaching a destination. It's also about the preparation that makes each next chapter of our life the greatest chapter.

Specific Struggles for Specific Purposes

Park rangers and Navy SEALs don't receive the same training. The demands of their duties require unique skills and unique shaping. In the same way, we each face different struggles that, if handled correctly, can prepare us for the challenging waters ahead.

Our journey isn't just about reaching a destination.

Struggles come from many different sources. Sometimes we bring them on ourselves, perhaps out of frustration or impatience or poor planning. A friend of mine flew to New Jersey for a meeting, where his plan was to rent a car and drive to his destination. The clerk working at the car rental desk was cranky, so my friend didn't say much. He did need directions, however, so he asked the clerk for a city map. "Above the visor!" the agent snapped. My friend found his car and left the lot. Once on the highway, he pulled down the visor. Sure enough, he found a map. It was a good map with clear directions. The only problem: it was a map of Chicago.

Sometimes struggles are born of past hurt, rejection, or other experiences in our relational histories. A counselor told me the story of a young married couple that came for marriage counseling. As a young boy, the husband had been dominated by his mother. It was no surprise that not long after his marriage began, conflict arose. Fed up with the push-back his wife was giving him, this young husband initiated a separation that led to divorce. The divorce may have had less to do with his wife than with his need to break free from his mother. Childhood pain frequently contributes to current struggles in life.

Struggle can also come from tests and trials. The biblical terminology used to describe trials is similar to that of a carpenter testing the strength of an object he's built. Let's say he builds a table held together with screws and glue. Once the glue is dry, the carpenter might twist the top with his hands, attempting to expose cracks or loose joints. He would listen for squeaks indicating the need for reinforcement. Much like that carpenter, God checks us for weak spots, exposing them with gentle yet firm pressure. When cracks surface, God can apply the necessary correction to make us strong for the next leg of our journey.

While God tests us to expose weaknesses so they can be strengthened, the devil's temptations expose our weaknesses so they can be exploited. Satan only wants to steal, kill, and destroy (see John 10:10). God will never tempt us, because it's not in His nature. He will, however, allow a weakness to be exposed so repairs can be made.

> God tests us to expose weaknesses and strengthen;
> the devil tempts us to expose weaknesses and exploit.

We learn in Scripture that Jesus was tempted. After a forty-day fast, He was hungry and weak. That's when the devil unleashed his first temptation. This is a common satanic tactic—to attack us at our weakest point. Repairing those weak points helps us move closer to our purpose. For example, learning early on in life how to deal with sexual temptation is a step toward developing a strong marriage. Or when financial weaknesses are exposed because of a limited budget, we learn how to be wiser stewards of our money for a future season when we're entrusted with more money.

The Bible tells us, "Behold, I have refined you, but not as silver; I have tested you in the furnace of affliction" (Isaiah 48:10, NASB). In the original texts, the word for "tested" can be literally translated "chosen." Through the refinement of suffering and affliction, God chooses us. God isn't impressed by the bullet points on our resumes. When He needs someone for a job, He looks in the furnace of affliction.

Lack of preparation can cause suffering. When proper paddling technique is used, the core body muscles drive the stroke. Novices who have not mastered the stroke often misuse their muscles and tire quickly. In life, well-meaning young adults sometimes do the same thing—pursuing their ministries and missions without first mastering the core disciplines. Disciplines like daily devotions, prayer, and planning are essential to an effective life. If we build our lives on a weak foundation, we will tire quickly and struggle unnecessarily.

Navigational errors also bring struggle. When a fiberglass canoe gets too close to a cliff, a powerful wave surge can crush it against the rocks. Proper navigation helps us to avoid those hazards. That is why it is so vital to be accountable to others: people can help us see hazards we might miss. It is also why we must be in daily communication, through prayer, with the Author of our purpose.

Growing Through Struggles

We attach value to all things in life by comparing one to another. Is family or work more valuable to us? Pleasure or obedience? Seasons of suffering allow us to reexamine the values we've given to these things. If you're on a hospital gurney with a life-threatening illness, the value of relationships will probably quickly rise above material things on your priority list. Facing eternity, we see that nothing is more important than a relationship with Christ. Suffering can bring our priorities into alignment.

Suffering should move us beyond good intentions to good actions. A life without struggle is usually a stunted life—a life without growth. The most stubborn of us will avoid struggle as long as possible, until the pain of staying where we are is greater than the action required to change or grow.

Sometimes we bring struggles on ourselves because we forget to measure our choices against what the Bible says. We fool ourselves into believing that if an action doesn't have any immediate consequences, it must be okay. One of the devil's greatest weapons is to withhold consequences. Why? How much do you think we'd sin if we always received instant consequences? The devil isn't interested in wounding us; he wants the kill. He wants us to become so entrenched in sin that escape seems impossible.

This scenario plays out every day. As a young husband begins struggling with pornography, the devil tempts him to hide the struggle. No consequences, right? Wrong. The man's inner life is constantly being damaged not only by the lie of pornography but also by the deceit required to keep his struggle hidden. He grows more and more distant from his wife. There are consequences, but he doesn't yet see them. Perhaps, in a moment of weakness, he acts out the fantasies, now indelibly written in his mind, with another woman. Once. Twice. Then the devil unveils the sin, the unfaithfulness, the infidelity. Cardiac arrest. Code blue. His marriage lies lifeless on the table.

When God exposes sin, He protects us from cardiac arrest. He protects us from the devil's plot to destroy us. When our choices bring pain, we must let Jesus deal with them right away. Sin doesn't destroy those of us who are believers—we all sin. But unresolved sin can destroy. When we run to God with our sins and struggles, we can be forgiven and set back on course.

A Matter of Perspective

God never wastes struggle. "You keep track of all my sorrows. You have collected all my tears in your bottle. You have recorded each one in your book" (Psalm 56:8, NLT). A well-traveled journey will not be one absent of pain but rather one that is right in the eyes of the Lord who prepared the journey. He examines us not for medals honoring our achievements but for scars of suffering—evidence of personal and spiritual growth.

God wraps His love around every aspect of our lives. That includes suffering.

God never wastes struggle.

Many of the struggles we face involve other people. How we relate to the suffering those struggles bring is a matter of perspective. "We get to decide whether suffering will make us better or bitter," Dr. Cordeiro often says. "Bitterness is like drinking poison and waiting for the other person to die."

I've been told that any time we have a problem with another person, we have a problem between God and us. When we view difficult people through God's eyes, we see them differently. We see that they have a purpose, a journey that is as important as ours. Perhaps theirs has been a difficult journey—one with a history of hurt. Hurt people hurt others. But when we choose to be bitter toward those who hurt us, we drink their poison over and over again.

We have the power to let go of pain, to ease our own suffering. Forgiveness is the source of that power. When we choose to forgive as Jesus did, we bring healing. Only through forgiveness can we stop the past from continuing to wound us.

· RECOVERY IN THE MIDST OF THE WAVES ·

The team quickly flipped the canoe back over and began to bail. Still in the water, we grabbed the ama and used our weight to keep the massive swells from flipping the boat again. In minutes the vessel was cleared of water, and we climbed aboard and paddled on.

As challenging as these moments are, we must learn to overcome them. We must learn to make adjustments and forge ahead no matter what the struggle or how it came upon us. Suffering handled poorly produces fear, which can paralyze us and cause us to miss opportunities meant to bless us. Courage is not the absence of fear but rather not allowing fear to take control.

When we struggle and suffer, we need to draw near to the One who created our journey and allow ourselves to be shaped and prepared for what lies ahead. God never promised our lives would be easy, but He did say He has overcome the troubles of the world and will never leave us. The reward of the journey far outweighs the struggle. When we suffer well, we join the ranks of those biblical heroes who went before us. When we let our struggles make us better instead of bitter, we move ahead into the greatness of our dreams.

JUMP IN

1. Name a time in your life when the devil withheld consequences until he could go in for the kill. What choices could you have made to foil his scheme?

_____

_____

_____

_____

_____

2. Forgiveness unlocks the chains that bind us to our pain. Some wounds leave deep scars that don't go away easily. How can you use the canoe-team metaphor to reshape the painful memories in your life?

_____

_____

_____

_____

_____

For further study, check out *Rising Above* by Wayne Cordeiro.

10

Seat 5—The Silent Force

S eat five is the silent force. This force is operational in all who are successful. Without it, even the most gifted individuals fail. I'm talking about daily habits and disciplines.

Nothing shapes life more than our daily actions. Many years ago, a consultant met with Japanese leaders to discuss ways they could improve their economy and products. He introduced a concept called *kaizen*. The essence of kaizen was to improve one thing about oneself every day. If corporations would improve just *one* trait of their organization each day, they would improve significantly over time. Japan is an economic powerhouse today because of this sort of thinking.

Our daily decisions lead to actions, which, when repeated over time, become habits. Habits shape our lives more than any other force. Good intentions are simply not powerful enough to overcome bad habits. We need to move beyond good intentions to good decisions. The Bible puts it this way: "Whoever keeps His word, in him the love of God has truly been perfected" (1 John 2:5, NASB). In other words, the love of God isn't perfected in desires, the heart, or good thoughts. It is perfected in action.

Enthusiasm for change won't matter
if you don't first get out of bed.

Perhaps you have the best of intentions to drop a few pounds. You just can't wait to hit the gym or get up early for that morning run. But all of that enthusiasm for change won't matter if you don't first get out of bed. We need to build a bridge over the chasm between good intentions and good choices. We do that by practicing what is right *regardless* of how we feel about it. (Right choices aren't always the easiest choices, or the most fun.) The Bible tells us that "solid food is for the mature, who because of practice have their senses trained to discern good and evil" (Hebrews 5:14, NASB). The word *practice* in this verse is similar in meaning to the word *echo*. It paints a picture of someone who repeats what he has seen—like Daniel-san mimicking Mr. Miyagi.

If we want to navigate our lives toward the greatness of our God-given assignments, we need to emulate the actions of those who are successfully navigating their purpose. We need to learn from their words and lives and train ourselves in the right way.

When we put down the DoubleStuf Oreos and put on our running shoes, that is moving beyond good intentions to action. The next step is to manage that decision, to make it consistent. Daily disciplines help us manage our choices.

My doctor, John Bryant, told me that the most effective physical exercise for my health is anything I do consistently. Running three miles a day might be a great workout, but running three miles once a month is *not* as beneficial as playing basketball every day for an hour.

Consistency takes commitment. And in this age of immediate gratification, commitment doesn't come easily. We want the benefits of a disciplined daily lifestyle but often don't want to do what's necessary to actually live it. We want thousands in the bank but don't want to work for the money. We want a faithful spouse but don't want to delay sexual pleasure. We want to see God do great things in our lives but don't want to pour ourselves into prayer or suffering like the heroes of the faith.

Becoming disciplined in life can be a painful process. Often it means giving up things we want, things that might satisfy a temporary desire. But here's one thing I'm sure of: any of these other pains is easier to handle than the pain of regret.

To achieve success, we need to learn how to faithfully endure the temporary pain that comes with choosing well. We need to discover the long-term benefit of delayed gratification.

• CLASS IS IN SESSION •

We are all enrolled in a class of higher learning. This class is taught by two excellent professors, both well versed in life and able to teach effectively. The first professor's name is "personal experience." We learn many of life's greatest lessons from our personal experiences and their consequences. For example, when you put your hand on a hot stove—and experience the consequence of pain—you learn, um, not to put your hand on a hot stove. Or maybe you choose to experience a lifestyle that's like some *Girls Gone Wild* video. I'm sure you can imagine some of those consequences. And some of the resulting pain.

The second professor's name is "others' experiences" or "others' wisdom." Much of this professor's greatest teaching is found in the Bible—in the lives of people like David, Solomon, Joseph, Moses, and Joshua. We can learn from their mistakes and see the consequences without actually experiencing their pain and suffering. How great is that? This second professor also teaches us through the lives of people like our parents, pastors, and other leaders and influencers.

> We can learn from their mistakes without
> experiencing their pain and suffering.

The difference between the two professors is great. To learn from the first teacher, from the consequences of your personal experience, you must first make a mistake. You must feel the pain and suffering before you learn your lesson. The wisdom of others, unlike personal consequences, allows

us to learn without first making a mistake. You'll learn from both professors in this life, but the more you can learn from others' wisdom, the fewer
roadblocks you'll run into along the path to your purpose.

· A NEW DAY ·

The buzzing of an alarm clock is often the first indication a new day has
come. After striking the snooze button a few times, we stumble to our feet
and race into our daily routine, leaping our scheduled and unscheduled
hurdles until we return home for the night. Then, after the alarm is set, we
sleep until that buzzer starts the cycle all over again.

Let me share a powerful concept a very wise man shared with me. It's
based on the creation of the earth.

> And God said, "Let there be light," and there was light. God saw
> that the light was good, and he separated the light from the dark-
> ness. God called the light "day," and the darkness he called "night."
> And there was evening, and there was morning—the first day.
> (Genesis 1:3–5)

Notice that God named the light "day" and the darkness "night." Then
God described the first day by saying that there was evening and morning,
the first day. A day, to God, *begins* with night. You might be thinking,
To-may-toes. To-mah-toes. What's the big deal, Danny? I'm glad you asked.
This is significant because it shows that life was designed to flow from rest.
Each day begins with evening, a time of rest. The activities that bring us
the most life flow from that rest.

Before we go to sleep, we should plan out the next day. Then our day begins with rest. Rest may be the most valuable of our daily disciplines.

· FIRST THINGS FIRST ·

I once heard of a college physics professor who gave a powerful illustration. Upon entering the classroom, students found a glass jar, five large rocks, and a container of sand on their desks. The professor instructed them to put all of the rocks and sand into the glass jar. Students used many different methods to fit all the material in their jars, all without success. When they had given up, the professor demonstrated the proper technique. First he placed all the large rocks into the jar. Then he slowly poured in the sand, shaking the jar from time to time to allow the sand to settle. In a few moments, the jar was full, and all the sand and rocks fit.

Rest may be the most valuable
of our daily disciplines.

More than offering a physics lesson, this story provides a life lesson, one that many highly successful people practice. In our daily planning, it's vital that we put the big rocks in our day first. These are activities that absolutely must get done. On any given day, your five big rocks may be prayer, devotions, exercise, dinner with family, and planning. They may be something else on another day. But the big rocks are those things most significant to our daily habits, those things that can best move us toward our God-given purpose.

To determine what your "big rocks" should be, ask yourself this question: What is God holding me accountable for in this season of my life? The answer to this question helps you uncover those things that are not important—those things you can eliminate from your life. And the answer can help you identify clearly what you need to accomplish each day to bring you closer to success.

Also, to accurately determine which are the big rocks, you need to take time to *think*. That's right—turn off the electronic devices, *including* the cell phone. Imagine what your future, family, life, ministry, and vocation might be. You can't put life on autopilot, sit back, and hope for the best. You must be intentional about drawing your map and then start moving in the right direction. Take time to think; then list the areas you know God is holding you accountable for. What daily activities do you need to do to make them happen?

After the big rocks are in the jar, then you can arrange the less important things around them. In this way, you can control the pace of your life, as well as the direction.

· THE BUCK STOPS HERE ·

Once we move from good intentions to good decision making, we must take action that keeps us moving forward. The initiative required for success is not automatic or issued at birth. We each must find what drives us toward our purpose and feed it. This is a challenge for members of today's younger generations. Many baby boomers grew up watching their parents struggle financially. They learned important life lessons from these difficult experiences and developed a strong work ethic to avoid a similar fate.

Driven to do better, they pushed through difficulty and developed a take-action attitude.

Gen Xers and millennials grew up reaping the benefits of the baby boomers' work and have more discretionary spending money than any generation in recent history. As a result, their decisions are less driven by a palpable sense of lack and often lead them to a motivation-free sense of false contentment or, at worst, entitlement. Members of this generation have to find inner motivation to push past comfort and become disciplined to reach their purpose.

Decisions about your daily routine, your habits,
and your pursuit of God are purpose-defining choices.

When making decisions about what's really important in your daily life, the buck stops with you. Indecision or a lack of motivation to learn and grow can cripple your future. Decisions about your daily routine, your habits, and your pursuit of God are purpose-defining choices. Make them wisely.

· A LIFESTYLE OF HONOR ·

One of the greatest ways we can practice good discipline in relationship to others is by showing honor. We have many opportunities in our workplaces, schools, ministries, and families to show honor. Honor is not the same as obedience. Obedience is the act of doing what somebody says to do and is usually the result of fear or respect. Showing honor, however, is much more than obedience. In the Bible, *honor* means "worth" or "value."

When we show honor, we do *more* than what's expected. We demonstrate that we value others by treating them with a good attitude. Honor asks us to consider the needs of others and act in ways that please them.

The apostle Paul gave this instruction: "Children, obey your parents in the Lord, for this is right. 'Honor your father and mother'—which is the first commandment with a promise—'that it may go well with you and that you may enjoy long life on the earth' " (Ephesians 6:1–3).

God included this command in the Ten Commandments, His foundational rules for living. Don't you find it interesting that along with "not murdering" is God's instruction to honor our parents? The Ten Commandments were not written to children. These lessons were for adults, so God has a special blessing for those who continue to honor their parents as they grow into adulthood. That doesn't mean we obey everything they ask of us—healthy boundaries are important for maintaining a good relationship with parents. But by honoring our parents, we can show that we still value them.

As we make good decisions that support the "big rocks" in our lives, we give strength to every other occupant of our canoe. Our gifts, attitude, and balance—combined with an ability to grow from struggle—propel us toward our purpose. With a heart of honor, we can soar to greatness.

JUMP IN

1. What are five of your big rocks—five things God is holding
   you accountable for during this season of your life?

   _____

   _____

   _____

   _____

   _____

   _____

   _____

2. What do you need to do each day to keep these big rocks
   prominent in your life?

   _____

   _____

   _____

   _____

   _____

   _____

   _____

3. What actions do you need to take to move toward your purpose?

_____

_____

_____

_____

_____

_____

_____

For further study, check out Pastor Wayne Cordeiro's lessons in leadership at www.MentoringLeaders.com.

11

Seat 6—The Steersman

Seat six provides the focus needed to finish the race.

Sitting high on the back of the canoe is a paddler with a different purpose. Unlike the other seats, this paddler constantly scans the horizon and water conditions to set the tempo for the vessel. The steersman's vision provides encouragement to the rest of the team while he guides the vessel from one navigational marker to the next. His eyes have been trained over the years to direct the vessel across the seemingly infinite terrain of the deep.

The steersman is equipped with a different type of paddle, which he uses to steer the canoe. He carefully examines many indicators and, based on his knowledge and experience, makes decisions to direct the canoe and the crew safely to the desired destination. The sixth seat is more than a lookout—this paddler must understand water conditions, tidal tables, and swell and wave dynamics.

We too need to train our eyes to see future rewards and not just stare at the current conditions. Our eyes must not be distracted by crashing waves but stay fixed on what's to come. The ability to focus can make all the difference.

A focused life is like a sniper rifle targeting
a very specific area with extreme accuracy.

A focused life is like a sniper rifle, which can target a very specific area with extreme accuracy. By contrast, an unfocused life is like a shotgun that throws many pellets in a general direction with much less impact. God designed us to have a deep impact in a specific area—the bull's-eye of our purpose. Like the steersman, our focused vision has one overarching goal: to guide us to the finish line.

• POWER OF THE IMAGINATION •

Vision can be defined as applied imagination. We all create things in our imagination before they materialize in the real world. Here's another way to look at it: memory examines the past, and our vision imagines the future. Vision is greater than anything our memory can recall, including our history, emotional scars, and failures.

We share the attribute of imagination with our Creator. Like God, we have the ability to create with our imagination. Everything you can see—computers, phones, pants, eyeglasses—was first imagined before it came into being.

We can use our imagination to create vision—to pursue our God-given purpose. In this way, our imagination can help us to do great things for the kingdom of heaven. But we can also use our imagination to pursue selfish pleasure. As Wayne Cordeiro puts it, "That's why Satan is a headhunter. His battlefield is your mind. His trophy is your imagination."

· THE FRONT LINES ·

God and Satan are battling on the front lines for our attention. Whoever owns your attention owns your vision too. Anything that captures and keeps our attention can control us. A psychology professor I respect, Adolph Brown, once told me that all that is necessary to teach someone a concept is to capture his or her attention. Consider that advertisers will spend more than $10 million producing a thirty-second commercial. Doesn't that say something about the value of our attention?

It's important to examine the voices that capture our attention. If you are consumed by thoughts of mindless entertainment, materialism, your image, sex, or selfish dreams, well, you know which side of the battlefield is capturing your attention. By the same token, if your thoughts are focused on fulfilling your life's purpose and developing your character, it's easy to see that God is winning the battle. The battle for your future is a battle for your attention—today. Whoever captures your attention most consistently...wins.

We've been examining all of the things we can do to fulfill our God-given purpose. What if we flip that idea for a moment? What does it take to destroy our future? How do you destroy the plans God has for this generation? Simple. Distract them from God's purpose: steal their attention.

· OUR ATTENTION DETERMINES OUR DIRECTION OF TRAVEL ·

What we look at and listen to affects the desires we have and, ultimately, the direction of our lives.

Author Ted Baehr recalls the work of Joseph Goebbels, the Nazi propaganda minister from 1933 to 1945. In his book *So You Want to Be in Pictures?* Baehr describes the account of Goebbels's effort to destroy Jews, evangelical Christians, handicapped Germans, and other groups of people through mercy killings:

> Finally, Goebbels produced a dramatic movie called *I Accuse,* an emotive feature film about a beautiful, intelligent woman who is dying of an incurable disease and begs to be allowed to commit suicide. After the movie was released, a majority of German people said they had changed their minds and now supported mercy killings. After a few more of Goebbels's films about invalids and handicapped people, the German people voted for mass mercy killings.[8]

Hitler worked in a similar way. Historian Paul Johnson writes in his book *Modern Times:*

Hitler appears always to have approached politics in terms of visual images. Like Lenin and still more like Stalin, he was an outstanding practitioner of the Century's most radical vice: social engineering—the notion that human beings can be shoveled around like concrete. But, in Hitler's case, there was always an artistic dimension to these satanic schemes. Hitler's artistic approach was absolutely central to his success. Historians agree the Germans were the best-educated nation in the world. To conquer their minds was very difficult. Their hearts, their sensibilities, were easy targets.[9]

No question—what we give our attention to does matter.

• OUR ATTENTION IS OUR INVESTMENT •

Our attention is an investment in the future. Whatever we have in our "life account"—our gifts, resources, time, energy, and passion—is what we can use to purchase our future.

If you were the recipient of a $100,000 gift, wouldn't it be wise to consider how you would spend it in light of the difference it could make for your future? How is our time any different? Knowing the power of giving attention to your future, how much more vigilant should we be in protecting that focus? We need to guard what we watch, listen to, play, or do and stay focused on the direction of our lives. After all, if the seats in our canoe are functioning perfectly but we're on the wrong course, we will not reach our destiny.

What has our attention also has our energy.

Imagine it's the middle of the night, you're sound asleep, and the phone rings. Adrenaline surges through your veins, and tragic thoughts flood your mind. You pick up the phone to hear an emotional voice telling you that a loved one has been in an accident and is on the way to the hospital. Do you hang up, roll over, and go back to sleep? Of course not! No matter how tired you are, you're infused with energy—your attention has been captured.

The steersman of your life is no different. As he scans the horizon, noting indications of trouble and navigational markers and making other observations, his responses and course adjustments energize the rest of the crew.

> If the seats in our canoe are functioning perfectly but
> we're on the wrong course, we will not reach our destiny.

It's been said that time is the currency of earth. We can lose money and make more, but we don't have that luxury with time. Time is life. When we steward our time wisely, we are literally stewarding our life wisely. The Bible instructs us to give our attention to what to do with our time: "Be careful how you walk, not as unwise men but as wise, making the most of your time, because the days are evil" (Ephesians 5:15–16, NASB). We live in a culture where marketers, consumers, and other interested parties compete for the prize of our time. Unless we strategically manage our time, we will slip into the default our culture sets. If we choose not to invest our time, we will spend it.

We need to carefully establish treasures to invest our time in that are consistent with God's purpose for our lives. We need to pray and ask God, *"Lord, what do You treasure? in my family? in my future? What do You see as valuable in my life?"* God wants to reveal these areas of our lives to us more than we want to know them. Write down what you feel God is sharing with you, and ask God to increase your love for those things.

"I don't have the time." When spoken about our purpose or God's treasures for our life, these five deadly words cause our dreams and purpose to go into cardiac arrest. We each make time for what we treasure and love. We make time for those we love, the activities we treasure, and the activities that we really want to be involved in. When we fail to do what we know is best or spend time on the things that we know are essential to a successful future, we need to examine what it is that we truly love.

Defaulting is easier than it may appear. Consider the fact that we each have 168 hours per week. Most of us spend 56 of those hours asleep. Between eating and personal hygiene, about 24 more hours disappear. Traveling to work or school and actual time at those activities consumes approximately 50 hours per week, leaving 38 hours. Do the math. Thirty-eight hours per week to invest leaves us with approximately 5 hours per day that we can invest in what we truly treasure. The default activities for those hours can quickly consume our greatest asset. The average American spends three of those five hours each day watching television. Video games, the Internet, and iPods can quickly move from entertainment to time-consumer if we are not careful to "make the most" of our time. Once it's spent, it's gone. Protecting our attention can help us make the most of every moment.

Six Steps to Protect Your Attention

1. Recognize that distractions destroy vision.
2. Train yourself to protect your focus. Only you can protect yourself.

3. Make wise decisions about music, media, and entertainment.
4. Starve wrong relationships. It only takes one person to destroy your future.
5. Pursue relationships that increase your focus on your purpose.
6. If it doesn't feed, fuel, or fertilize positive focus, forget it.[10]

· CAPTURED BY GOD ·

Anything that steals our attention can negatively affect our mobility. But when we're focused on God, we will move in the right direction. Look at Isaiah's experience encountering God:

In the year that King Uzziah died, I saw the Lord seated on a throne, high and exalted, and the train of his robe filled the temple. Above him were seraphs, each with six wings: With two wings they covered their faces, with two they covered their feet, and with two they were flying. And they were calling to one another:
"Holy, holy, holy is the LORD Almighty;
      the whole earth is full of his glory."
At the sound of their voices the doorposts and thresholds shook and the temple was filled with smoke.
"Woe to me!" I cried. "I am ruined! For I am a man of unclean lips, and I live among a people of unclean lips, and my eyes have seen the King, the LORD Almighty."
Then one of the seraphs flew to me with a live coal in his hand, which he had taken with tongs from the altar. With it he touched

my mouth and said, "See, this has touched your lips; your guilt is taken away and your sin atoned for."

Then I heard the voice of the Lord saying, "Whom shall I send? And who will go for us?"

And I said, "Here am I. Send me!" (Isaiah 6:1–8)

When Isaiah's attention was captured by God, he obtained a clear sense of the vision God had for him. Seeing God high and lifted up changed his perspective.

I have two incredible sons. Neither one is an alien. They are human. I didn't try to make them human. They are human because I am their father and they have my DNA. In the same way, we are like our heavenly Father, made in His image. Just a glimpse of our Creator can inspire us to passionately pursue our vision.

Recognizing Vision

Vision has the ability to keep us on course. Proverbs tells us, "Where there is no vision, the people perish" (Proverbs 29:18, KJV). The New International Version words it: "Where there is no revelation, the people cast off restraint." Vision comes from understanding our purpose. It is the ability to see the end from the beginning. You may be new to knowing your purpose or even caring about it. Maybe you are seeing some markers ahead and have the general idea for navigation. Where you are isn't nearly as important as where you are headed. Vision will help you see that destination from wherever you are today. Vision can be described as an ability to perceive something not visible through foresight. Good thing God gave us

His attribute of imagination—without it we wouldn't be able to see past the nose on our face. But with it, and God's guidance, we can learn to see far off into the distance.

Recognize and Promote "Vision Allies"

There are positive voices all around us that can help us stay on course, that can help clarify our vision. We find these voices in good friendships, pastors, parents, music, books, and activities that help us grow closer to God. Take the time to promote and protect those voices in your life. This is why a strong prayer and Bible study time is such a vital daily habit. We have no better ally in our search for clear vision than the One who created us and prepared our journey.

· VISION + GIFTS = PURPOSE ·

The combination of your unique gifts and your vision set the plan of action to achieve your purpose. The gifts you've been given—and what you do with them—will prepare you to reach each goal along the path to your purpose. How do you know you're heading the right way? That's what vision is for. It points you toward God's ultimate purpose for your life.

Without that vision, we would float haphazardly around the ocean, living from one moment to the next, perhaps moving from pleasure to pleasure, but without a destination. With vision we can learn how to use our gifts and abilities to steer toward God's intent for our lives.

Without vision, we will wander the earth, lost and confused. But with our God-given vision, we will navigate confidently into the purpose for which God has created us.

JUMP IN

1. What are the strongest competitors for your attention?

_____

_____

_____

_____

2. What steps for protecting your attention do you most need to take?

_____

_____

_____

_____

3. Who are some of your greatest "vision allies"?

_____

_____

_____

_____

4. Who are some of your greatest "vision enemies"?

_____

_____

_____

_____

_____

5. What decisions can you make today to begin distancing yourself from those enemies and drawing nearer to your allies?

_____

_____

_____

_____

DESTINY

12

Season Yourself

S easoned paddlers make the best canoe team members. Not only are seasoned paddlers stronger than inexperienced paddlers, they also have better balance and intuition. Through training and failure and time-consuming trial and error, they've developed their abilities and even a "sixth sense" that gives them an edge over other teams.

As with any sport, mastery of the fundamentals is essential to becoming the best. Mastery of the foundational skills in canoeing—rowing, leaning, counting—makes the difference between winning and losing, between a champion and everyone else. The team that wins the most often is the one whose members have refined their foundational skills. The same is true in pursuing your life purpose.

> The team that wins the most often is the one whose members have refined their foundational skills.

Here are seven foundational character skills that, when mastered, can propel you with excellence into your life purpose.

· FOUNDATIONAL SKILL 1: TAKE INITIATIVE ·

Wayne Cordeiro talks about a foundational class we each need to take that you won't find in any course catalog: initiative. We must seek help to discover our unique identity, and to do that we need to take the initiative to find mentors who can help us discover our most vital characteristics.

Mentors don't typically appear in your life until you're ready for them. Your readiness creates a hunger to learn from a mentor's wisdom and experience. It's your job to learn from the brightest and wisest mentors if you want to avoid common pitfalls and achieve exceptional results. Mentors reward initiative generously with their time and insight. If you take the first step of finding a mentor, you will reap rich benefits.

A mentor you can spend time with is invaluable to your foundational development. But you can also learn from experts and leaders you can't meet with. Many public figures, past and present, have tremendous wisdom, but that wisdom is only available to you through stories in the media or written works. With a little research and initiative, you can learn about leadership from Abraham Lincoln, about commitment to a cause from Joan of Arc, or about generosity of spirit from Mother Teresa.

When we study the deep character of those who have gone before us, we reap the great rewards of their wisdom.

• FOUNDATIONAL SKILL 2: CREATE TRUST •

No matter what roles we play in life, trust is the key to becoming excellent in those roles. We each have blind spots, and it often takes a trusted friend to reveal them to us. Pride makes it difficult for us to reveal heart issues like jealousy, unforgiveness, pain, or fear, but good friendships enable us to honestly examine these parts of our lives.

Unfortunately, trust doesn't come easily. Developing trust takes time. And trust is fragile; it can be shattered by harmful words, condescending attitudes, and manipulative actions. Broken trust can damage and even end friendships. But when we work on our people skills and our emotional intelligence, we protect that trust—the most important element of strong relationships. We must be careful to apply good judgment, integrity, and servanthood in situational aspects of life if we expect to move forward with excellence. We must learn to be faithful with the small things if we want to be entrusted with more.

• FOUNDATIONAL SKILL 3: BE TEACHABLE •

Take a good look at your life. Consider your abilities. Your skills. What do you see? No matter how good or bad you feel about these areas, this one thing is true: if you're not teachable, this is the best they'll ever be. Unless you are willing to learn from those who have been where you are, you won't grow and you won't improve. Being teachable takes humility. Jealousy, resentment, and pride can squelch your ability to learn. But if you listen to wisdom, study God's Word, and are quick to address problems, you can grow your abilities and skills and become a "seasoned paddler" more quickly.

• FOUNDATIONAL SKILL 4: NEUTRALIZE YOUR CHARACTER ENEMIES •

Anything that threatens the development of our true character is an enemy.

You may get impatient along your journey. In that impatience, you may react with unwise choices, rushing in too quickly, overeager to validate your own ideas and desires. Doubt sets in when questions arise about your character. And though these periods of doubt can be instructive, it's important to exercise patience when struggling through times of questioning.

Remember, there are no shortcuts to greatness. The lure of shortcuts creates some of the worst struggles for many young people. Our potential can only be developed by applying our character in everyday situations. Unless we're committed to the daily work, even our strengths can become enemies.

Remember, there are no shortcuts to greatness.

There is one enemy of greatness that is particularly dangerous and devious. It is odorless, invisible, and usually undetectable to the one possessing it. I'm talking about pride. A healthy self-image is a powerful force for proving our character, but pride lies in wait on the other side of a healthy self-image. Pride makes us weak.

The poison of pride feeds off our fears: *What if I'm misunderstanding God about this? If I do that, what will my friends say? What if I look stupid?* The motivator behind these questions is pride refusing to be corrected, warping our vision, and causing us to put ourselves first. The temptation to appear secure can become a subtle game of one-upmanship.

When sewer plant operators inspect sewer systems, they wear an indicator to warn them against deadly gases. This is because the operators have become so accustomed to the odor that they can't recognize when the gas is at a dangerous level. Without the warning indicator, their lives would be at great risk.

This same concept applies to pride. We can't detect pride by ourselves because we become accustomed to its existence in our life. Trusted friends who know our habits become our indicators—they can hold us accountable and alert us when our pride level rises to dangerous levels.

If you're struggling with dangerous levels of pride, humble yourself and ask others for help.

· FOUNDATIONAL SKILL 5: PRUNE WELL ·

As we discussed earlier, margins are essential to maintaining a healthy balance in life. A life without margins is often plagued by anger, hostility, and loneliness. Being busy doesn't make us valuable.

Think of a healthy tree that has enough sap for one hundred branches. If that strong, normal tree grows four hundred branches, not all the branches will develop properly. The result will be a fruitless, withered tree.

What a vivid picture of a life without margins. As healthy and productive people pursuing our life purpose, we sometimes forget about margins. We fill our lives with responsibilities, duties, and relationships that dilute the effectiveness of our sap. When that happens, the areas that need to be healthy suffer as our resources are diverted from one growing limb to another. The secret of fruitfulness isn't adding things to our lives but rather pruning wisely. Pruning isn't the random chopping off of limbs, however. First we must determine which branches are necessary. God gives us just the right amount of sap for everything He desires for us to do.

> The secret of fruitfulness isn't
> adding things to our lives
> but rather pruning wisely.

But which branches do we cut? The answer comes when we spend time with the One who designed us. Grab a pen and a notebook and ask God, "What am I accountable for in this season of my life?" Write down the answers and pray about them. Soon you will know what's important.

After we cut back what's unnecessary, our specifically designed abilities can grow according to God's unique design. It would be easy to shape our lives according to a design that worked well for someone else. But while it's good to learn from the wisdom and life lessons of others, it's important to remember that each of us is completely unique. When pruned back to our individual uniqueness, we will discover a renewed energy and vitality. Fresh growth will come to the existing branches.

The Three Steps of Pruning a Healthy Character
1. Seek your unique design.
2. Discard false impressions about yourself.
3. Use your specific talents every day.

· FOUNDATIONAL SKILL 6: ESTABLISH INTERNAL ANCHORS ·

What keeps you tethered to who you really are when the world's temptations come knocking?

Every day we are tempted to fulfill flesh-based desires. When we were growing up, our parents may have provided anchors for us through discipline and boundaries. Yet as we launch from the mother ship, we need new anchors. Some of these will be internal anchors based on what our parents gave us. But once we leave home, developing these internal anchors becomes our responsibility. And the earlier we establish them, the better. Whether we glean wisdom from our parents, the Bible, or the experiences of others, we must establish anchors to keep us on course in turbulent waters.

· FOUNDATIONAL SKILL 7: DEVELOP DISCIPLINE IN DEVOTIONS ·

The most important foundational skill is a daily devotional life. Spending consistent time with God not only helps us detect pride but also gives us the wisdom to make good choices on a daily basis. Wouldn't it be nice to avoid the painful consequences of bad decisions?

The Bible is a collection of sixty-six books filled with advice and life experiences from some of the wisest people who ever lived. Isaiah tells us the Word of God "stands forever" (Isaiah 40:8). No other text or manual can claim to be reliable for all generations. God's Word can make you wiser than your age. The psalmist writes:

> Oh, how I love your law!
>   I meditate on it all day long.
> Your commands make me wiser than my enemies,
>   for they are ever with me.
> I have more insight than all my teachers,
>   for I meditate on your statutes.
> I have more understanding than the elders,
>   for I obey your precepts. (Psalms 119:97–100)

Here's a deep thought: not only can we study the Bible but the Bible studies us! The Word opens our hearts:

> For the word of God is living and active. Sharper than any double-edged sword, it penetrates even to dividing soul and spirit, joints and marrow; it judges the thoughts and attitudes of the heart. Nothing in all creation is hidden from God's sight. Everything is uncovered and laid bare before the eyes of him to whom we must give account. (Hebrews 4:12–13)

It's a great idea to write down what God is showing you. The best journaling tool I have found is the Life Journal (www.lifejournal.cc) created at New Hope Christian Fellowship in Honolulu, Hawaii. This plan helps you study Scripture, make observations, and apply them to your life. Journals for adults, youth, and kids are available at https://resources.enewhope.org/store/.

13

Finish Well

We have a race to run: our Christian life. And we have a goal: our God-given purpose. Finishing well means running well, and that requires a commitment to improvement and excellence.

In Hebrews 11 we read about great men and women of the faith who ran their race with excellence. They were people just like you and me who stepped off the shore and accepted God's invitation to the deep. Though their lives weren't easy, they accomplished their purpose with such excellence that their stories are forever a part of the eternal Scriptures.

Joseph, Abraham, Moses's parents, Noah, Rahab—the list is long and includes some people who were brutally murdered for their faith. These men and women ran their race differently than those around them. Their commitment to an eternal purpose made them stand out, even among other great men and women of their day. What was their earthly reward? They didn't get one. "And all these, having gained approval through their faith, did not receive what was promised" (Hebrews 11:39, NASB).

That's right—during their lifetime—zip, nada, zilch. No reward.

What's with that? I thought our God was a God of love. He is. The Hebrews passage continues: "Because God had provided something *better* for us, so that apart from us they would not be made perfect" (v. 40, NASB).

What kind of race were they running? A sprint? A marathon? I think the best image is that of a relay race. A relay race hinges on successfully passing a baton. If the baton is dropped, the team's chance for success drops dramatically. These godly men and women listed in Hebrews 11 ran their race well and then passed the baton of faith to others. Many generations have done the same. Today we are carrying the baton. How will we ensure a smooth pass to the next generation?

How we finish our race and fulfill our purpose
impacts much more than our own lives.

The Bible wasn't originally written with chapter breaks (they were added later to help readers navigate the texts). So continuing into Hebrews chapter 12, we read, "Therefore, since we have so great a cloud of witnesses surrounding us, let us also lay aside every encumbrance and the sin which so easily entangles us, and let us run with endurance the race that is set before us" (v. 1, NASB). In Paul's way of thinking, it's almost as if at least some of the reward granted to those great men and women who went before us is wrapped up in how *we* run our lap.

Think about it. In a relay, runners give their best for the team, spurred on by the person who handed them the baton. In the same way, we are motivated to run faster and better by those who have gone before us. They ran well. They've left you a legacy and inspiration. So I ask, how are you running?

Daniel prayed when he knew it would cost him everything. He ran well. David Livingstone died on the mission field in Africa. His African converts removed his heart and buried it in Africa before his body was returned to England because "his heart was for the people of Africa." He ran well too. Many who have gone before us have run well. How we finish our race and fulfill our purpose impacts much more than our own lives. Our actions are the fulfillment, in part, of other believers' rewards.

• ELIMINATE OBSTACLES •

Committing to this powerful legacy is the first step toward finishing well. But one step isn't enough. Champions are forged in the discipline of day-to-day training. When we get up early in the morning to journal and study the Bible, we are training to become champions. When we serve at church or reach into life's gutter to share love with someone others shun, we are learning to run like champions. The cloud of witnesses cheers wildly when we run well.

Daily training helps us throw off the hindrances of sin. Instead of asking,

"What can I get by with and still get into heaven?" we ask, "What can I get rid of to help me run stronger? Which relationships draw me closer to my divine purpose? Which ones distract me?" We need to patrol our hearts and ask, "What attitudes do I have that are harmful to my life? Do I have fear, pride, bitterness, or a need to forgive someone?" These sins can entangle us if we aren't training regularly in righteousness.

Champions recognize the significance of these obstacles and work to eliminate them through consistent practice. Champions move beyond good intentions to good habits.

· FORGET COMFORT ·

Olympic athletes take every aspect of their training seriously. The apostle Paul puts it this way:

> Everyone who competes in the games goes into strict training. They
> do it to get a crown that will not last; but we do it to get a crown
> that will last forever. Therefore I do not run like a man running aim-
> lessly; I do not fight like a man beating the air. No, I beat my body
> and make it my slave so that after I have preached to others, I myself
> will not be disqualified for the prize. (1 Corinthians 9:25–27)

Those who finish well fix their eyes on the "author and perfecter" of our faith (Hebrews 12:2). This focus makes all the difference. Jesus's objective isn't providing for our comfort but rather perfecting us.

A while ago, I started going to a gym to get into better shape. I knew a little about weight training, but my physique didn't particularly show evidence of that knowledge. One night I decided to try for a new goal on the bench press. I had never lifted that much weight, so I needed a spotter, someone to make sure I didn't hurt myself. I scanned the room and saw a large, muscular man nearby. In my deepest macho voice I asked, "Can you give me a spot?" He walked over and leaned over the bar as I got into position, unaware that I was about to be challenged to my core.

> "I beat my body and make it my slave…"

I slid on my Walkman's headphones, cranked up the mix tape, fixed my hands on the bar, and lifted it off the supports. It was then I noticed the letters on my spotter's hat, which even upside down I could clearly make out as "USMC Drill Instructor." *Gulp.* It was too late to turn back now, so I pressed one slow lift and went for a second. I strained to push it beyond halfway. At that moment, the drill instructor leaned his bald head over me, dripping sweat onto my forehead. He fixed his eyes to mine and screamed, "Push! Push! Push! You will not quit, boy!" Everyone in the gym had stopped their workout to watch the little weakling being yelled at by the big bald guy. But my attention was captured by the drill instructor, and I grunted out a raspy "Yes sir!" and magically proceeded to crank out reps I didn't realize I had in me.

Before my spotter showed up, I didn't have my eyes on the goal. And even when I started my lift, it wasn't until the instructor challenged me that I was able to see beyond the relative comfort of one or two reps to a greater goal. The goal in working out isn't comfort—it's progress, growth. But if we let our eyes wander toward what's easy, we'll never reach beyond comfort. As canoeists, we must fix our eyes on the navigational markers ahead. As runners in a relay, we must focus on running our lap with the baton in the shortest time possible. And in our race toward our purpose, we are to fix our eyes on Jesus Himself.

Sin and pride will always try to trip us up. This is why it's so important to establish boundaries and protect our focus. The enemy's goal is to steal, kill, and destroy. And when he can't destroy, he'll distract—get us to trade our purpose for pleasure, riches, or fame. He would love for us to drop that baton.

· ENSURE THE PASS ·

Those who finish well make a smooth pass of the baton. To make a clean pass of the faith to the next generation, we must remain focused on what each step requires. Paul wrote:

> To the weak I became weak, to win the weak. I have become all things to all men so that by all possible means I might save some. I do all this for the sake of the gospel, that I may share in its blessings. Do you not know that in a race all the runners run, but only one gets the prize? Run in such a way as to get the prize. (1 Corinthians 9:22–24)

We ensure a smooth pass when we train daily, fix our focus, and eliminate obstacles. We know that even as we're pursuing our purpose, it's not about us or where we've been or what we will accomplish. It's about the baton we carry here and now—the message of faith, in the gospel of Jesus

Christ. We can craft meaningful legacies of faith *even* in times of crisis. No matter how our lap around the track is going, we can finish well.

One day we—like Paul, David, Moses, and Joshua—will cross the finish line. When we leave this world and enter the next, we'll have run our laps; we'll have done our part according to God's purpose. Until that day, let us carry the baton in a way that is worthy of the runners who have gone before.

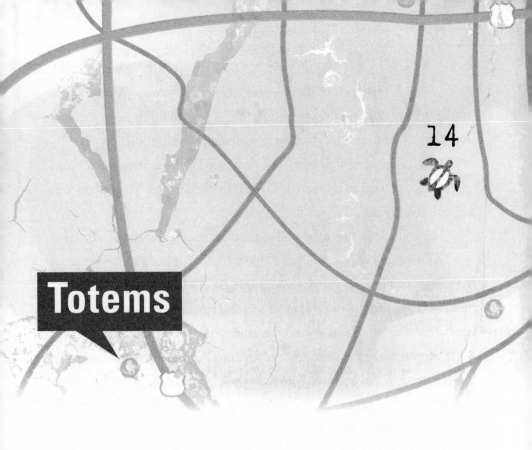

14

Totems

Certain traits appear consistently in the lives of great men and women who finished their races well. These traits stand out as *totems*—representations of the characteristics that became keys to their success.

Native cultures used totems to inspire future generations. Totems were like crests, portraying unique attributes about a family—attributes that were essential for mastering life challenges and ensuring survival. When creating the combined totem pole, village elders gathered and asked, "What traits do people in our village need to grow up with?" They would agree on the most important characteristics, which were represented with icons:

"Conditions are rough here. They will need to be as strong as a bear."

"They will need to respect the subzero thermal winds. That will require strength like an eagle."

"The wild climate changes will require the resourcefulness of a badger."

These images were carved into a pole that was placed in the center of the village for all to see. Parents would interpret the images for curious children, teaching them about the attributes that made their people strong and what it took to survive in a harsh environment.

There are no totem poles where I live. But I can't help wondering, what if there were? What if people who knew how to successfully navigate their life's purpose had carved totems to help the next generation? What would those carved images tell us?

Here are some totems I would stack in the center of my village.

· TOTEM 1: CHARACTER ·

It was Christmastime, and I was looking for a special gift for my wife. I found myself in front of a fine jewelry store owned by a friend of mine, a gemologist named Nick, who loved to show me his high-end stock. He would open the safe and show me brilliant jewels and stunning settings. He'd let me hold diamonds valued at more than $40,000. I would look at these flawless rocks and think, *How dangerous to actually wear one of these...*

I recalled a time when my wife told me about an emerald that kept falling out of one of her favorite rings. It made me wonder if there is any setting secure enough to protect one of those incredibly valuable diamonds in Nick's store. In *Gems Along the Way,* Wayne Cordeiro compares the setting of a ring to personal character. In this book, written for his children, he says a ring's setting doesn't get nearly as much notice as the gem. Yet the setting is crucial to the jewelry.[11] Nick would never entrust a precious gem to a setting with weak prongs. The gems God has planned for us on our journey need a strong setting too—they need a strong character to support and hold their value.

The value of a strong character is inestimable.

The value of a strong character is inestimable. Think of relationships. A strong marriage isn't built on flimsy prongs of feelings, attractions, or fleeting romance. It is built on the solid character of two committed individuals.

Think of finances. Your character is what determines whether your prosperity will be squandered on fleeting pleasures or stewarded wisely to bless others and to help fuel your greater purpose.

Think of status. You may be promoted to greater levels of service because of your gifts and abilities, but how you handle that promotion is dependent on your character. Does pride set in? Do you begin to disrespect people and try to sabotage them? Or do you remain humble and kind?

Character is the all-important setting for the valuable gems of life.

• TOTEM 2: CREDIBILITY •

The word *credibility* comes from the Latin word *credo,* which literally means "to believe in, to have faith or trust in." Those who successfully navigate their purpose are committed to following through on what they promise. They are reliable men and women. They apply skills, communication, and a positive attitude to achieve ever-increasing levels of trust with the people in their life.

Trust is an essential component in every relationship. Whether in a friendship, a marriage, a ministry, or a team, trust solidifies the connection and makes growth possible.

When people sense we are hiding something from them, we damage trust. Yet when we communicate openly with others, trust grows. Honesty is the fuel of trust.

True credibility cannot be purchased or taken from others; it must be earned. Consistently living our convictions and life principles lays a foundation of trust on which credibility can be built. When we build on that foundation with such things as respect, generosity, kindness, encouragement, selflessness, and confidence, others will come to know us as credible, trustworthy people.

• TOTEM 3: PLANNING •

A carefully crafted plan is one of the greatest secrets to success. You've probably heard this little nugget of wisdom: failing to plan is planning to fail. Well, it's true. We can't live our lives randomly and expect a successful outcome.

Picture a school of two thousand students somewhere on the East Coast. If each student got into a car, left the parking lot, and made random right and left turns for twenty-four hours, what would be their chances of arriving at Niagara Falls? Slim to none. But this is exactly what we do when we fail to plan.

We know from the Bible that God is a planner.

Some people believe that planning is contradictory to being led by the Spirit. These people wait for a "sign from God" before they take action. I'm not saying signs from God are a bad thing—it's important to be open to God's divine intervention in our lives. But we know from the Bible that God is a planner. Did He come up with that idea of Jesus dying on the cross at the last minute? I don't think so. No, God plans. And He expects us to do the same.

The psalmist wrote, "Teach us to number our days aright, that we may gain a heart of wisdom" (Psalm 90:12). Keeping track of our days—planning—brings wisdom. Wisdom is just one benefit of planning. When God directs our lives, He makes use of our plans. As the Bible says in Proverbs, "The mind of man plans his way, but the LORD directs his steps" (16:9, NASB). If we don't plan, what does God have to direct? He shows us how to navigate the deep. He allows our choices to prove our faith and then uses our plan as He directs.

When we take the time to plan, we reap a more balanced life. We learn to better prioritize our time and keep urgent needs from controlling us. Planning reduces the chance of exceeding our margins. Planning sets us up for success. Planning inspires others to follow our lead. Have you ever walked a path in the dark? It's tough to convince people to follow you if you're walking without insight. Our plans may not be perfect, but God can refine those plans, aiming us closer to the bull's-eye.

Your ultimate goal as you pursue your purpose is to get know your Creator and to pour His love into the world.

Finally, planning makes it more likely we'll make it to the finish line. Let's recap four basic life-planning steps:

1. Write Your Goals

Know what you're trying to accomplish. Know your vision and your purpose. Then plot the best course to get there. Choosing the right goals will ensure that your time, energy, and other resources will not be wasted.

2. Seek Mentors

Whether you're looking for a career, an ideal, or a particular characteristic, find mentors with specific, useful knowledge to help you in your search. Find someone who's in a vocation or ministry like the one God is leading you toward. Then interview this person—ask lots of questions and soak up his or her life-lived wisdom.

3. Focus Your Resources

Make a list of resources you will need to execute your plan. Maybe you'll need a second job and tighter stewardship of your money. Perhaps you'll need to rework how you budget your time. Don't forget the importance of margin.

4. Be Realistic

Don't expect a plan to work if you've failed to appropriately assess your situation. Even as you're setting goals and making a plan, remember that life isn't about the destination. Your ultimate goal as you pursue your purpose is to get to know your Creator and to pour His love into the world. Put the big rocks in the jar first, and seek balance in your journey.

• TOTEM 4: EMOTIONAL INTELLIGENCE (EQ) •

Studies of successful people reveal that IQ alone is not a good indicator of leadership success. A more commonly shared characteristic among the successful is what I like to call Emotional Intelligence (EQ). As I mentioned earlier, we were not designed to fulfill our purpose alone. Our life calling will inevitably involve other people. The difference between success and failure in life often hinges on how skillfully we work with others.

In ministry or the workplace, poor interpersonal skills lower overall efficiency and effectiveness by eroding motivation and replacing it with apathy and hostility. However, EQ traits like teachability and positive relational skills can greatly improve your chance of success. Teachable people have an easier time adapting to change and can grow and improve by accepting advice or correction. And those who have good relational abilities, like sensitivity to others' circumstances, patience, and good listening skills, create synergy and inspire growth in both individuals and teams.

It only takes two minutes to make a first impression. However, according to experts, reversing a first impression requires a whole lot more than two minutes. A high EQ and knowing who you are and what you bring to the situations you face is the key to confidently presenting a good first impression.

Another factor that can hinder success is the inability to handle pressure well. Self-control is a vital component of emotional intelligence. Being able to remain composed under stress and calm in the face of inevitable conflict goes a long way toward building a successful life. People who struggle in this area are prone to reacting defensively. They deny accountability, cover up failure, and blame others. Overly aggressive, abrasive, arrogant people who lack empathy will also struggle to achieve success. Those who display tact and diplomacy do well.

> A high EQ is the key to confidently
> presenting a good first impression.

Esther, Daniel, and Joseph all had high EQs. I believe this was an important factor that led to God's favor. God grants His divine favor when we exhibit a healthy EQ and use it for His purpose. God honors our commitment and dedication.

There are many other totems I could list here. Some I've already mentioned, including a positive attitude, vision, courage, passion, and problem-solving skills. Study these totems. Ask your Father in heaven to interpret them for you. And model your life after what you learn from those who have successfully navigated their course.

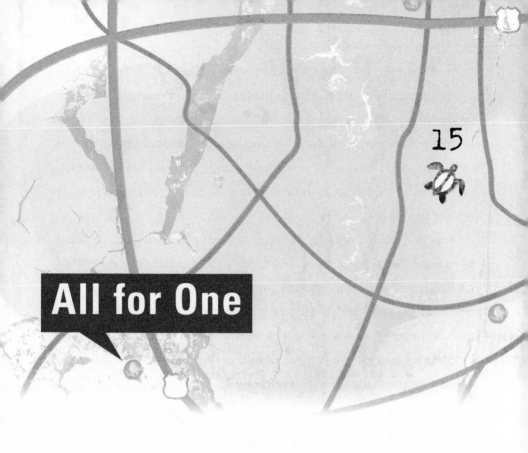

All for One

15

Y ou are here. You stand on the shore, overlooking the deep blue of the unknown. You are about to take a seat in the canoe. Perhaps you're wondering, *What's next?*

Be encouraged. Be confident. When you decide to push off into the deep in pursuit of God's purpose, God does not leave you to fend for yourself. He is right there with you.

And remember—it's not about the destination; it's about the journey. The greatest memories will come from moments along the way. That is where God will reveal glimpses of true beauty. The journey teaches us, perfects us, and allows us to participate with heaven in God's great plan. It allows us to partner with those who've gone before, to carry the baton into the world.

Your purpose is uniquely important to God's plan. You have the potential to touch hearts and change lives. Don't paddle timidly into that potential. Reach for it with every stroke. Give it your best. How many graves hold unpainted masterpieces? Underneath that green sod, was there hope for someone hurting? was there healing? was there encouragement? Go to the grave having given all you've got. Commit to the hard and rewarding work of discovering and fulfilling your purpose.

> Your purpose is uniquely important
> to God's plan.

Your generation needs what God has placed inside you. Right now people are praying for your gift to reach into their lives. From the beginning of time, you were designed to be God's answer to those prayers.

Will you join me on the water? Take hold of the paddle passed on to you, fix your eyes on Jesus, and head for the prize.

Ride the waves of opportunity.

All of eternity awaits your finish.

Paddle hard and finish well.

ACKNOWLEDGMENTS

Thank you to: *Amanda*. In 1994 we began our journey. It has been filled with excitement and joys as well as sorrow. I have learned so much by your side, and the journey to greatness as a man of God and a husband seems to have just begun. Our moments of joy and regret have shaped me. Areas I have excelled in and others where I have fallen short have challenged me to the core. Oh, how I wish the journey were easier. I wish every moment was like the gift of a bouquet of freshly sharpened pencils on a cool fall morning in New York City, a massage amongst the gently crashing waves at Turtle Bay, or the sand between our toes as we cuddled together at a Ko Olina lagoon, watching a famous Hawaiian sunset. As much as those images have painted our memories and dreams, they have not shaped us as much as our journey into the deep. The path behind us has been mixed with experiences that brought the deepest joys and sorrows. Many of these I would never want to see either of us experience again. But as I look at the horizon, my attention is captured and I am indebted to God for His goodness in not allowing us to remain the same, in refining us for His glory. Thank you for walking with me, as difficult as some of those places were.

Joshua and Caleb. You are the two most incredible boys any father could be blessed with. This book was written with you in mind. It was my dream to write it from the first day I held each of you in my arms.

You are growing up so quickly, and very soon you will be living the words of this book. You will stand on the shore of greatness and step into the most incredible life you could ever imagine. God planned out every day of your life before time began, and I can see how great you both will be. Remember, you are not alone. God is always with you, and your mother and I will be by your side cheering for you as you experience the joys and sorrows of your journey. We will spend countless hours having "Boys Day Out," golfing, and catching waves. And when you feel like you are in over your head or don't know which way to go, know that you are not alone. I believe in you both and will love you unconditionally, no matter what! You were placed on this planet to do incredible things, and I am already so proud of the great men of God you have become. I can see God's hand on your life, equipping you to do something very special that will bring Him great glory. Never forget you were created for greatness. It's truly an honor and privilege to be chosen by God to be your father, and an even greater honor to be called "Dad." I love you more than you will ever know.

Pastor Wayne. Thank you for being my pastor, mentor, and friend. I have been amazed by your wisdom and leadership. The "DNA" you have imparted to me bleeds through the pages of this book. The countless hours I have spent in front of the screen of my Mac feverishly typing words based on your wisdom and guidance have taken this book to a level I never would have been capable of accomplishing alone. I wish every reader had the opportunity to be shaped by you. You are a voice this generation must hear. I thank God for the opportunity to include in the pages of this book some of the content you had for my life. You have set the bar high for me, and for that I am indebted.

Pastor Elwin. I have never met anyone like you. When I sit and talk with you, I could be face to face with Solomon. I sense your wisdom and leadership without your speaking a word. You are redefining for this generation what a man is supposed to be, and your leadership raises the bar well beyond the norm. My life is richer because I know you and have allowed you to shape me. Thank you.

Notes

1. Dan Miller, *48 Days to the Work You Love* (Nashville: Broadman and Holman, 2005).

2. "Passing the Baton," a live training presentation developed by Dr. Jeff Myers, www.myersinstitute.com.

3. Wayne Cordeiro, *Attitudes That Attract Success* (Ventura, CA: Regal, 2001), 17–18.

4. Cordeiro, *Attitudes That Attract Success,* 42.

5. John C. Maxwell, *The Winning Attitude: Your Keys to Personal Success* (Nashville: Nelson, 1996), 162.

6. Adapted from Miller, *48 Days,* 61–64.

7. Pat Robertson and Bob Slosser, *The Secret Kingdom* (Nashville: Nelson, 1987), 161–162.

8. Ted Baehr, *So You Want to Be in Pictures? A Christian Resource for "Making It" in Hollywood* (Nashville: Broadman and Holman, 2005), 81–82.

9. Paul Johnson, *Modern Times: The World from the Twenties to the Nineties,* rev. ed. (New York: HarperPerennial, 1992), 130.

10. Adapted from Mike Murdock, *The Assignment: Powerful Secrets for Discovering Your Destiny* (Tulsa, OK: Albury, 1997), 35–36.

11. Wayne Cordeiro, *Gems Along the Way* (Honolulu: New Hope, 1997), 74–75.

ABOUT THE AUTHOR

DANNY HOLLAND has studied youth culture professionally for nearly two decades, traveling across the nation and the world, talking to thousands of young adults. Danny is an internationally sought-after speaker and author, and when he's not speaking, he can be found with his two sons, Josh and Caleb.

Visit www.DannyHolland.com for more information about Danny's itinerary or to contact him.

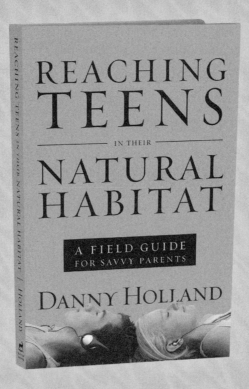